DISCIPLINE = POWER

How to Master Self Control, Build Better Habits, and Achieve Your Goals

By: Devin White

ALL RIGHTS RESERVED

No part of this book may be reproduced, stored in a retrieval system, or transmitted in any form or by any means, electronic, mechanical, photocopying, recording, scanning, or otherwise, without the prior written permission of the publisher.

Limit of Liability/Disclaimer of Warranty: the publisher and the author make no representations or warranties with respect to the accuracy or completeness of the contents of this work and specifically disclaim all warranties, including without limitation warranties of fitness for a particular purpose. No warranty may be created or extended by sales or promotional materials. The advice and strategies contained herein may not be suitable for every situation. This work is sold with the understanding that the publisher is not engaged in rendering medical, legal or other professional advice or services. If professional assistance is required, the services of a competent professional person should be sought. Neither the publisher nor the author shall be liable for damages arising herefrom. The fact that an individual, organization or website is referred to in this work as a citation and/or potential source of further information does not mean that the author or the publisher endorses the information the individuals, organization or website may provide or recommendations they/it may make. Further, readers should be aware that websites listed on this work may have changed or disappeared between when this work was written and when it is read.

Table of Contents

Introduction 1

Chapter 1: The Big Secret 5

Chapter 2: Building Discipline Muscles 12

Chapter 3: Failure Is Not an Option 20

Chapter 4: Athletes and High Achievers 25

Chapter 5: Goal Setting Secrets 33

Chapter 6: Deflating Obstacles 41

Chapter 7: Intention and Attention 48

Chapter 8: Using the Power of Discipline 58

Chapter 9: Celebrating Every Step 73

Chapter 10: Confidence vs. Overconfidence 84

Chapter 11: Accountability Wins 95

Chapter 12: Muscle Memory 103

Chapter 13: Momentum Theory 108

Chapter 14: A Slippery Slope 113

Chapter 15: The Discipline to Try Again 122

Chapter 16: Being Vulnerable 127

Chapter 17: What Winning Looks Like 134

Chapter 18: Discipline Mastery 141

Conclusion 155

Introduction

Remember the first time you tried to ride a bicycle? That sense of fear and uncertainty never leaves us. Suddenly, it was as if a miracle occurred. You tried once more - pushing your weight down on the pedal and suddenly, you felt yourself propelled forward with enough gusto that gravity didn't push you to the ground. You did it! You conquered something that you didn't know you could.

What gets us to the point where we become determined? Did you take one more chance at riding your bike because the neighbor boy, who's twice as clumsy as you, learned to do it? Did you come to the conclusion that there was no way that your older sibling learned and you were going to fail?

Whatever it is - there's real value in that type of determination. Let's bottle that and use it when we need it most. Like right now!

I understand why you chose this book. I wrote it because I thought the same things you're thinking: "If only I had more discipline I could accomplish _____. You are obviously motivated because you care about discipline. You also made a good choice because I'm going to teach you to ride the discipline bike. You're older now, so you fear failure in a way that you didn't as a child. That's an obstacle that we can, and will, overcome.

My motivation for writing this book was both generous and self-serving. I wrote this book for my children because I wanted them to learn about the power of discipline. Anything powerful can be scary, especially when we don't understand it. And anything powerful can be wonderful if we can harness it. By many measures, I've been a successful business leader for more than 20 years. Twice I've built and sold businesses. I've hired, trained, and motivated others to become leaders - and I can tell you that there's no better feeling than to see someone you've empowered rise up through the ranks of leadership. To rise up and become a leader requires a certain amount of discipline, but not an inordinate amount.

No one is perfectly disciplined. Pick out someone you think I've overlooked in making that statement. Someone who you know is hyper-disciplined because you can see the evidence. The chiseled bodybuilder, the accomplished musician, the CEO of a Fortune 500 company. If you think these types of people harness the power of discipline, you're right, but to varying degrees. If you ask any one of them about their discipline, they'll tell you that they are extremely disciplined in that area of focus that matters to their success in their given field of expertise. It doesn't mean they clean every plate in the sink before they go to bed, or that they can eat just one Oreo.

As you'll see in the chapters to come, discipline and focus go hand in hand. Discipline and motivational factors too.

If you seek to become a more disciplined person in order to achieve a certain goal, I guarantee you that the discipline you want is available to you. All it takes to attain it is understanding how to first acquire the mindset and habits that foster discipline.

This book will give you the tools to change your relationship with discipline. You'll learn strategies for making commitments to yourself that you can keep. The pages that follow will unlock the secrets of becoming more disciplined and you'll gain motivation that makes it easy. Lastly, you'll discover how to become more focused, mindful and present.

Here's some great news: you can not fail at discipline. Sure, you may be disappointed at your consistent inability to *stay committed* to a practice that you believe to be important to your success. That doesn't mean you should define yourself and your ability by those experiences. They're in the past - just like your inability to ride a bicycle that preceded the onset of that ability!

If you've recently brushed your teeth, shown up to an appointment on time or washed and folded laundry - you are not undisciplined. It took a degree of discipline to accomplish any of those tasks. You have the muscle. You just need to implement a practice that strengthens it.

This is good news. You are most definitely not a failure at discipline. You have a busy life, in a noisy and often confusing world - like the rest of us. Your inability to maintain focus on creating the habits necessary for success have only eluded you "so far." Words have power. Remember that the past only has the power over you if you allow it. If there's something important to you that you've not achieved so far, that's all it is, something you haven't mastered *yet*.

As you read this book, take your time to stop and reflect, but try to refrain from dwelling on anything from the past. Building new habits is something we can do in the present and the future only. This mindset is important. It sets the groundwork for us to create powerful outcomes.

Together, we'll connect the neurons in your brain that make the discipline you crave become attainable - so that you can master self-control, build better habits and achieve your goals. Your power awaits. **Let's begin.**

Chapter 1: The Big Secret

"Success isn't measured by money or power or social rank. Success is measured by your discipline and inner peace."

– Mike Ditka

Discipline gets a bad rap. Here are some terms the Merriam-Webster dictionary uses to define "discipline" as a noun:

- Control gained by enforcing obedience or order
- Orderly or prescribed conduct or pattern of behavior
- Training that corrects, molds, or perfects the mental faculties or moral character

The verb "discipline" is described with these terms:

- To punish or penalize for the sake of enforcing obedience and perfecting moral character
- To train or develop by instruction and exercise especially in self-control
- To impose order upon

Is it any wonder that we may have a psychological resistance against embracing something that has such potentially violent connotations?

Here's the best news I can share with you. **Discipline need not be any of these things.**
How we define discipline helps to define our relationship to it.

Redefining Discipline

Thinking of discipline as an "orderly or prescribed conduct or pattern of behavior" is certainly not enticing. "Control gained by enforcing obedience or order" sounds like something you might want for a well-trained pet, but not something you're too keen on "enforcing" upon yourself.

It seems pretty obvious that if we view discipline as something other than wonderful and powerful then we're setting up obstacles for embracing it. Often, such obstacles are present in the unconscious mind and they sabotage the development of good habits that are sustainable.

The big secret is this: we have the power to define discipline in a way that is more inviting, more motivating. In doing so, we create the framework for establishing a positive relationship with this powerful behavioral practice.

On New Footing

With a strong foundation in place, we find ourselves on new footing with discipline. Once we define it as we wish, it's no longer that thing that belongs to marathon runners, early risers and dessert avoiders. If we define it, we can own it. If we can own it, we can master it.

What do we do with this newfound power? We do what powerful people do: we create! It's time to define discipline in a way that fuels our ambition. We need a brand of discipline that empowers us to create and stick to the habits that allow us to reach our goals. Here's a neat trick. Let's begin with the end in mind. Let's take a look at our goals and reverse engineer our definition of discipline. We'll define discipline in terms that allow it to be the tool we need. The tool that helps us adhere to healthy habits. The type of habits that enable us to reach our goals.

Goals First

Grab a piece of paper, or since we live in the digital age, create a clean Word doc, Google doc or whatever tool you use to create a list these days. **Pick three high priority goals** and write them down. Be specific so that they can easily be visualized - something that's hard to do when we reference something that's vague.

If your goal is to lose weight, put down how many pounds, specifically. If your goal is to learn a computer programming language, define which one. If your goal is to cut down on alcohol consumption, go further to determine whether the goal is to: stop for a month; not exceed two drinks on any given day; refrain from drinking during weekdays; refrain for the rest of your life - the more specific the better.

If performing this task requires you to do some research or soul searching - do it - because the more closely you can define your goals, the better.

Actions Required

Now that you've defined your goals, think about the actions required to achieve them. If your goal is to learn to play a specific song on the piano, think about three things you can do to facilitate your ability to achieve it. Here's an example of three actions you could take to reach this goal:

- Commit to spending five hours per week practicing.
- Spend two hours a week reading about music theory
- Allocate one hour per week to watching piano technique videos on YouTube

If your goal is to abstain from doing something, think about actions that are a replacement or substitution - so that you are saying "yes" to something you want - and not simply denying yourself. While removing an unhealthy or unwanted habit should be motivation enough, saying "yes" is typically more motivating than saying "no."

Take a moment now to **list three meaningful actions** for each goal. These are actions that, when taken, will demonstrably move you closer toward reaching the goal that's in focus.

Mindset

With goals and actions in place, now we can address what puts the wheels in motion. Where do we draw our strength? If we believe, as the title of this book suggests, that discipline = power - where do we find the motivation to be disciplined.

Without such motivation, how could we possibly achieve today what we've failed to achieve thus far?

So much of what determines our success in anything, including our ability to be disciplined in taking actions that help us reach our goals, is our approach. I've always loved this famous quote from carmaker Henry Ford:

"Whether you think you can, or you think you can't - you're right."

With this in mind, our approach must begin with a can-do attitude. And, at the risk of circular thinking, this brings us back to "what's my motivation?" and "How can I trust myself to follow through this time?"

The answer lies in our perspective. Do we see actions we defined as actions we need to take or actions we want to take. Making a choice is always more inviting than being compelled to do something. Let's agree to not look at the actions we've defined as chores or tasks - just as we don't view the goals we've set for ourselves as anything but positive. Why should we need to go through a series of negative actions to get to a positive result?

One way is to create a mindset that turns our actions into events in which we are fortunate to be, rather than compelled to do, is by maintaining focus on our tangible goals.

Power over Discipline

Here's the secret: we're going to own discipline. The power belongs to us - not to "discipline" - the characteristic that we've been unable to master so far. The way we take our power over discipline is to define it in a way that attracts us, rather than repelling us.

Let's look at what we are reverse-engineering: Goals - Actions - Motivation - Mindset - Discipline.

The way to create a mindset that turns our actions into something we're fortunate to do, rather than compelled to do, is by maintaining focus on our tangible goals.

We Define Discipline

Discipline is the power one owns to make good on the promise to oneself.

What's the Difference?

Our definition is empowering. We already own the power, it's within us. It's based upon a promise we made to ourselves. These ideas are positive.

It's a definition that is related to the original ones, but it's far different from one that "forces obedience or order" or "prescribes conduct or pattern of behavior." It's even further removed from some sort of "training that corrects, molds, or perfects the mental faculties or moral character."

In the form of a noun, you'll come to see that ours is one that carries less resistance in our subconscious - and that may be all the difference we need.

The verb "discipline" is something we can ignore altogether. In the context of our definition, there is no room to "discipline" another being as a way of punishing, penalizing, training or "imposing order upon."

The power of discipline exists within the concept of what it is; that which we can master and from benefit from its presence.

Chapter 2: Building Discipline Muscles

> "I've learned over the years that freedom is just the other side of discipline."
>
> – Jake Gyllenhaal

Now that we have a definition of discipline we can relate to, be inspired by, and draw strength from, it's time to build discipline muscles. What are discipline muscles, you ask? They're a metaphor for strengthening our brain's ability to see discipline differently.

Like muscle training, we can implement exercises that strengthen our new relationship with the power of discipline.

In the physical world of building muscle, you do so by exercising the muscle strenuously - so that you break down the fibers - almost as if you're damaging the muscle. Of course, the human body is incredibly resilient, so what happens? The body rebuilds the muscle bigger and stronger.

Here's some good news. There's no strenuous activity involved in building discipline muscles.

Let's do an exercise together. This one focuses on the goals you choose.
Here we go:

1) **Pick a goal.** It could be one you listed while reading the previous chapter - or a new one - whatever inspires you most right now.

2) **Describe why you chose this goal.**
   - What are the benefits? Think in the grandest terms how achieving this goal makes you feel about yourself

3) **Visualize goal achievement. Use your senses.**
   - What does achieving this goal look like?
   - How does it make you feel?

4) **Post-achievement goal assessment.**
   - Does achieving this goal leave you feeling satisfied?
   - Is this goal a stepping stone toward another goal or the final step in an evolutionary process?
   - Do you feel more powerful?

Here's one example of how this exercise might look completed:

1) **My goal is to lose 20 pounds..**

2) **Describe why you chose this goal.**
   a) I want to be healthier
   b) I want to look better dressed
   c) I want to look better undressed
   d) I want to feel more attractive
   e) I want people to see me as more disciplined

3) **Visualize goal achievement. Use your senses.**
   a) I can imagine what my stomach looks like flatter
   b) I can feel how my shirt hangs from shoulders and hangs without resting on my belly
   c) I can sense the feeling of being more lean - a feeling I've had before and I like it
   d) I can imagine the compliments I'll get from friends and family

4) **Post-achievement goal assessment.**
   a) I'll feel mostly satisfied. Not totally because I think I need to lose more than 20 pounds to be at my healthiest and best-looking weight.
   b) This is a great step toward getting to my ideal weight.
   c) Achieving this goal definitely makes me feel empowered. I'm proud of myself for keeping the promise I made to myself.

Just as with physical exercise, completing a set feels good. You can feel your brain being stimulated and know that you're progressing toward a stronger YOU.

Since we're warmed up and our blood is flowing, let's do another. This time we'll focus on the actions you choose to help achieve your goals.

Here we go.

1) **Pick an action that propels you toward your goal.** Again, you can pick one you listed while reading the previous chapter - or use a new one.

2) **Describe why you chose this action.**
   - How does performing this action move you closer to achieving your goal, specifically?

3) **Consider your mindset.**
   - What frame of mind do you adopt to perform this action well?

4) **Visualize partaking in this action. Use your senses.**
   - How do you feel when you take this action?
   - What are the sounds and other sensations that accompany this action?

5) **Action completion assessment.**
   - Does completing this action leave you feeling satisfied?
   - Once completing this action, do you feel more powerful? If so, why?

I'll share an example of an action related to my goal to lose 20 pounds.

1) **Running is the action I'm taking to help me lose 20 pounds.**

2) **I chose running because it's an effective tool for burning calories.**
   - Running is an efficient way to burn calories quickly.

- It also has other benefits, including heart health achieved through cardiovascular workout and muscle building, which helps metabolism.
- I've previously taken up running for the purpose of losing weight, and it's proven effective for me. Incidentally, the same has proven true for me with partaking in a walking routine, but with running I simply can achieve the results faster.

3) **My mindset is determined and must overcome certain fears.**
    - To begin a running routine, I must do some planning to help me address certain fears.
    - My fears include the *fear of quitting* because certain days I won't feel like running (I know this from previous experience).
    - I reduce my fear of quitting by reminding myself that this is a choice I'm making. It's to help reach a goal. I'm choosing running because I like the benefits and I know that after I complete my first few runs, it begins to have a magnetic effect, where my desire to go for a run outweighs my concerns about such things as, "will I get tired and not be able to run as far as I want to, and then feel like a failure."
    - I know that fear of failing is what stops me from taking certain chances, and I'm almost always rewarded handsomely for overcoming that fear and taking a chance.

4) **Running feels great and it gets me outside, into a natural setting.**
    - I think about how good it feels to run. I have a sense of gratitude that I'm physically able to run - even though I can't run as fast or as far as I did years ago.
    - I remember that the joys of running outside include being out in nature - passing trees, seeing the sky, and hearing birds chirp as a I run. It's a nice part of the experience of this activity.
    - I remember how good it feels to sweat. How good it is for your body to release toxins through your sweat glands.
    - I consider the mind clearing effects of running - the way running can help me put my thoughts in order - and when in a good rhythm, it's much like meditating.

5) **Completing a run feels great.**
    - There is a great feeling of satisfaction from completing a run. It's the completion of an action taken to achieve a higher goal - but completing each run is completion of a goal too.
    - Each run I complete makes me feel powerful. I've committed to do something and by following through, I've reinforced to myself that I have the discipline required to keep a promise that I make to myself.
    - The sense of achievement I get from completing a run typically stays with me for at

least the rest of that day, and sometimes it lasts longer.

If you're a runner, or ever have been, you probably relate to the experience I've outlined. Yet these same parameters can be applied to any activity. From painting to reading a book, to finishing a music lesson - each leaves us better than we started - closer to a bigger goal. Each requires a certain mindset to create the forward movement needed to being and the determination to finish.

It's easy to see how mindset is so important. The right mindset turns a chore into a privilege.

A positive mindset provides us with a "can do" attitude. A mindset that includes self-compassion tells us it's okay to have fears of failing, but that we can create a plan where we can't fail. We can't fail if we believe that trying is succeeding. And we can always try!

QUICK NOTE: In case you're this thought crossed your mind: "If this guy is so knowledgeable about discipline, why isn't he already at his ideal weight?" It's a good question. The answer is: we're all human/ None of us are disciplined all the time in all areas of our life. This is true of the Olympic athlete, the concert pianist, and the Rhodes scholar. We are all human, so perfection is not a reasonable option, but excellence is. Discipline is about focus and attention. When we master discipline, we can apply it when and where we choose. Our ability to maintain it in any given area of life is determined by our motivations. That's why this book is longer than Nike's "Just do it" slogan.

Does taking a "deep dive" on these activities make you feel motivated? It does for me. I'm off for a run. See you at the beginning of the next chapter.

Chapter 3: Failure Is Not an Option

"Don't worry about failures, worry about the chances you miss when you don't even try."

– Jack Canfield

This quote best sums it up best. The opportunity in front of us, to harness the power of discipline, is out of reach of our fear of failure is greater than our desire. Every great achievement this world has ever known began with inspiration. Achievements are only possible when inspiration is allowed to grow into a plan, and that plan is enacted upon. Worry is too often the emotion that extinguishes inspiration.

What can we do about it? First, we have to acknowledge that fear is the elephant in the room. It's what causes us to stop before we start, or quit earlier than expected once we've started. Fear is failure's best friend. When we get fear to work for us instead of working against us, we can defeat failure once and for all. If you're like me, you're thinking, "I hate fear and I'm tired of fear getting in my way." That's the spirit.

The problem with fear is that it knows how to hide in plain sight, sneak up on us, and catch us when we're most vulnerable. When we feel tired and worn out, we don't always have the energy to fight fear, so we give in. That's when our fear turns to failure, and as we know, failure can cause us such pain that we stop wanting to try something new just so that we can avoid it.

Here's the great news: we control our minds, so we can prepare a plan that helps us be ready for fear. If we anticipate it, we won't be surprised, and when we are armed with a plan, we will have the strength to fight and defeat fear when it confronts us.

Making Friends with Fear

"I don't want to be friends with fear," says just about everyone. Making friends with fear doesn't mean we're going to pal around together. We're not going to have dinner, watch a movie, or show up to a party with fear next to us. Making friends with fear just speaks to the fact that we need to have a working relationship with fear. A relationship that works for us.

The way our minds work can be tricky at times. This is especially the case when it comes to resistance. The more we resist something, the more power it has over us. It's natural to have thoughts you wish you could repress, but have difficulty doing so. Whether it's a failed relationship, a missed opportunity or any other painful memory, the best way to deal with it is
"to deal with it."

When we tell ourselves that we're simply tired of thinking about a painful memory, so we'll just not think about it, it doesn't typically work if we haven't come to a resolution about it. The human brain doesn't do well with unresolved issues.

Whether we like it or not, we may be able to push issues out of our conscious brain for a while, but we have no say about the unconscious part of our brain. Our unconscious brain has its way of pushing those unresolved issues right back into our consciousness.

For that reason, let's iron out our differences with fear. In doing so, we'll create a structure that allows us to move past fear and avoid failure.

Game Plan to Combat Fear

Old school thinking about discipline would tell us to be goal-focused, keep our eyes on the prize, and that would provide a road to success. What's missing from that simplistic thinking is that there are reasons for why we find goal-oriented success to be fleeting. There's a reason why sometimes we have success in harnessing the power of discipline and other times we can't summon the strength to maintain focus.

Fear is usually what derails us. Like I alluded to earlier, fear and failure are close pals. To defeat fear, we need to anticipate how, when and where it may appear. Preparation is the key to success. So, how do we prepare for fear? The same way winning teams game plan for the opponent, we prepare for fear by considering how it shows up for us, based upon past experiences. We game plan by creating a strategy of tactics we can use to defeat fear. If our strategy is correct, when fear shows up, acknowledge it, focus our attention and face it head on.

Our best tactics for defeating fear draw upon our goal-oriented motivations. We are always stronger when saying "yes" to positive than "no" to a negative. When fear shows up, we're prepared because we have a mindset that draws power from our mission - the initial promise we made to ourselves. Think about the promises you've made to yourself that matter most. Those promises empower you to be bold, to put yourself out there, to go for it!

Having a positive mindset is great, but what do we do to keep focused? If you've lived through the 80s or have since seen the movie Ferris Bueller's Day Off, you may remember this famous quote spoken by Ferris, "Life moves pretty fast. If you don't stop and look around once in a while, you could miss it." Point being, it's easy to lose focus on what matters most to us. Life does indeed move pretty fast. And that movie was made before the internet made mobile phones and social media what it is today. See, now I've lost focus. Oh yeah, the point is focus. We need tools to keep what's most important top of mind.
Think creatively for a moment about what tools you could employ to stay focused on something that you deem to be life altering (Crazy right? You'd think something life altering would always stay top of mind).

Here are some ideas:
- Use your mobile phone's calendar and/or alarm functions to set reminders about your mission, your motivation, the commitments you make to yourself.
- Leave sticky notes in strategic places. This may sound silly, but it works.

- Use the "Schedule send" email feature to send emails to yourself - that show up at future times in your email inbox.
- Ask a friend to remind you. You may even want to be mission buddies - where you remind each other about your missions

The bottom line is that a plan is all you need to ensure that you're focused enough to ensure that you are consistently trying. As Winston Churchill is often credited with saying, "He who fails to plan is planning to fail."

Bring On "Failure"

Failure is not an option because we have the ability to define failure narrowly, as the equivalent of *not trying*. Conversely, as long as we try, we cannot fail. We know that the primary reason to quit trying is related to fear of failure - and that's a fear that we overcome with a positive, prepared mindset.

Promise yourself that you'll tap into the power of discipline because your motivations are more important than fear of failure, or any other obstacle that may present itself. When we are supremely focused on making good on the promise we make to ourselves, failure is not an option. Let's learn more.

Chapter 4: Athletes and High Achievers

> "It's hard to beat a person who never gives up."
> – Babe Ruth

It's only natural to think that Olympic athletes and other elite achievers are different from the rest of us. In one respect that's true. In another, it's completely false. Let's start out with why it's false.

We'll never know for sure what degree of high achievement is due to the valid arguments on both sides for "nature versus nurture."

For every story about an athlete whose natural gifts appear to be supernatural - with regard to characteristics such as strength, speed and intelligence - there are as many stories, or more, about people who rise above the competition because of sheer desire.

If you look at the incredibly successful New England Patriots football team, you need look no further than two of their star players to see great examples of how work ethic, more than raw talent, make them great. Tom Brady is often referred to as the GOAT, which stands for Greatest Of All Time, for his achievements at the quarterback position. He's the only player to have won the Super Bowl six times.

As current and former teammates, coaches, other NFL players and analysts describe what makes Tom such a great player, they routinely describe his work ethic and his desire to win. In other words, effort is what makes him great. This is an important revelation because it illuminates that anyone who puts forth a great effort can achieve a high level of success. It's important to realize that effort and determination contribute greatly to the motivational factors and mindset we've spoken of so far.

While playing for the New England Patriots between the years of 2000 and 2019, Tom Brady and his coach, Bill Belichick, were by far the winningest team in the National Football League.

Here's how Coach Belichick describes Tom Brady:

> "He wasn't all that good when we got him. He mechanically wasn't anywhere near where it eventually has ended up. Nobody's worked harder than Tom. He's trained hard. He's worked hard on his throwing mechanics. He's earned everything that he's achieved."

Coach Bill Belichick has suggested that Tom's success is attributed to three traits: 1) A strong work ethic; 2) The ability to think strategically; and 3) His ability to focus and stay "in the moment." Once again, these are qualities that are universally available, so this tells us that anyone who values these qualities and is willing to work hard can similarly achieve his or her own lofty goals.

If you want to make a counterpoint argument about Tom Brady, you might point out that he also has certain physical attributes that allow him to play at this high level. For example, he is six feet four inches tall. To that point, someone else could point out all the other 6'4" quarterbacks who don't make it to the NFL at all, and the many who do that never achieve even a small percentage of what Tom has accomplished.

Hard Work Pays Dividends

One Tom Brady teammate who won three Super Bowls with him is a wide receiver named Julian Edelman. Julian is undersized for an NFL player in that position. He stands 5'10" and the league average for a wide receiver is above 6'1", with many of the elite players in that position at the high end of the spectrum. In the wide receiver position, height can be an especially useful tool for getting an advantage over a defending player.

How did Julian Edelman become a receiver in the starting lineup year after year on the best team in football? Experts will tell you that it's because Julian's work ethic, determination and focus are so strong. Julian Edelman was a seventh-round draft pick when he made it into the NFL. By all accounts, he worked harder than the competition when it came to working out in the weight room, on the practice field, and during the off season to ensure that he was as fit, fast, agile, and durable as he could possibly be.

Julian has three Super Bowl rings to signify his achievements and was named Most Valuable Player in the 2019 Super Bowl game. It's worth celebrating the achievements of someone who works hard because it points to the power of discipline. When we speak of determination, work ethic and focus, we're talking about motivators and mindset that foster the discipline to accomplish goals.

Preparation Is Paramount

In the previous chapter, we spoke about being prepared to face fear so that we can be sure to stop it in its path and not let it lead to failure. In the context of goal achievement, preparation is what goes into having the right mindset for success. It also relates to the cascading nature of goals - how one goal is the predecessor for another.

Getting prepared is an action that moves us toward goal achievement. Think about physical exercise. Trainers and coaches stress the importance of a warm-up routine - so that there's a new rate of blood flow and muscle warmth before moving on to something strenuous. Warming up is preparation for the exercise about to commence.

Preparation begins even earlier. If you head off to the gym to exercise, or a field, you prepare, right? You may bring a water bottle, perhaps a towel to dry your sweat, and maybe even a change of clothes depending on where you're headed next. As important as it is to be prepared so that you have what you need to succeed physically, our mental preparation is even more important.

Without mental preparation, we're simply not showing up at the gym, the playing field, to work or anywhere else. To have the discipline to seize our power to achieve something, we always begin with mental preparation. With regard to the Discipline Hierarchy of Needs, mental preparation is strongest when we're conscious of the promise made to oneself, the goals created to fulfill that promise, the motivations that create a winning mindset and the actions to be taken to move toward goal achievement. We are always at our strongest when these elements are aligned.

Be a Gym Rat

I'm not sure if you're familiar with the term, "gym rat," but let's begin by understanding that it's a metaphor and a positive attribute. It's a term you may hear applied to a basketball player who works hard at her game. If she shows up early to get extra practice in, and stays late to continue working on shooting, dribbling, and endurance training - that's a gym rat.

Tom Brady and Julian Edelman are both known to be at the practice field early and to stay late. Julian Edelman is certainly described by people who know him as a gym rat in the offseason because he spends so much time in the weight room and performing cross-fit exercises.

This term can easily be applied to any other act of determination. If you're striving to get good grades, do the extra work that ensures you are giving it your all. The same holds true if you're in a job at work. Being a gym rat serves you in a number of ways. If you've made a promise to yourself to work hard to achieve your goal, being a gym rat, doing the extra work, helps you know that you are doing your best. Doing the extra work helps you achieve your goal faster than you would with less effort put forth.

One more benefit of being a gym rat is what you demonstrate to those who take notice. This has nothing to do with "being a poser." By a poser, I mean the type of person who wants you to think that they are working hard, but they're really just posing - in other words - they're faking it. What I'm talking about when I say "getting noticed" is that your hard work demonstrates to others your commitment, your discipline. So powerful is discipline that when we act in a disciplined way, people do take notice. It's impressive to see someone willing to work hard to get what they want.

In the case of the athlete who is a gym rat, her teammates, trainers and coaches take notice and it may win her a starting position or more playing time. The competition may also notice, whether they've heard rumors about her competitiveness or can see her chiseled muscles - she may benefit from the psychological advantage gained from others knowing that she's a gym rat - she's determined!

Universally Applied Traits

Legendary football coach and motivational speaker Luo Holtz said, **"Ability is what you're capable of doing. Motivation determines what you do. Attitude determines how well you do it."**
I like this quote for a number of reasons. First of all, it describes ability in terms of potential. That's an important distinction. What you're able to do and what you actually do

are two different things. To maximize your ability in an area of life that interests you sounds like a pretty solid goal that we should all choose. I like that Lou speaks of motivation as the determining factor of what you do.

You'll never make it to the office, the practice field or classroom if you're not sufficiently motivated.

The last part of the Lou Holtz quote above is really powerful. It's attitude that determines how well you perform. You've heard me speak quite a bit about mindset. Mindset and attitude are very closely related. Some people might consider them to be the same thing. I see them as just slightly different. I see mindset as more of the foundation of the frame of mind that allows you to feel a certain way.

In order to feel happy, you need a mindset that's optimistic and content. That feeling of happiness stems from optimism may lead you to have a confident attitude. The interesting thing about motivation is that while it may be what contributes to your attitude, your attitude can also fuel your motivation. When you have an attitude of confidence, it's easier to be motivated to take risks - and we know that sometimes we have to take risks in order to reap a reward.

Whether we use sports metaphors, business analogies or personal improvement examples, it's clear that successful people have certain traits that we can observe and apply to anything we wish to accomplish.

Good habits are a prime example. Athletes and high performers create and adhere to good habits. It's part of the process. Having a process and believing in it - that following the process will lead you toward goal achievement - is common among high achievers. Many of them preach, "Trust the process" for this reason.

Our ability to trust the process, create good habits, and foster a "can do" attitude all hinge upon our ability to harness the power of discipline.

Chapter 5: Goal Setting Secrets

> "People with goals succeed because they know where they're going."
>
> – Earl Nightingale

Most likely, you are reading this book because you want to have more control over your actions, your ability to meet commitments and your ability to achieve your goals. Goals are tricky. Set one too lofty and you risk falling short of attainment. Set one too low and you lose out on opportunity. The opportunity to do something bigger, and worse yet, the opportunity to be more excited, nervous, and motivated. Reward and risk go hand-in-hand, and nowhere does that feel more tangible than when you're sitting at the crossroads of goal setting.

Let's take a step back and remember that the goals we set are actually aligned with a higher yearning. That higher yearning may be a promise we make to ourselves or simply be in tune with something we believe about ourselves. Goals are almost always set, in order to prove something to ourselves - or about ourselves. When you set a new goal, consider your higher yearnings and investigate which higher need may be acting upon you. Likewise, examine an already established goal for the same type of connection - being cognizant of the connection may strengthen your ability to reach the goal.

Sweaty Palms Are a Good Thing

Setting a lofty goal should get you heart racing. That's when you know that you are in the right zone of loftiness. As discussed earlier, set a goal with clear results in mind, nothing vague. Don't set a goal to lose weight, set a goal to lose 15 pounds. If losing 15 pounds doesn't get you to your target weight, consider increasing the size of the goal. You can always celebrate milestones along the way. In the lofty goal setting stage, really push yourself. It's okay to choose a goal that you don't know whether or not you can reach it. In fact, that's pretty much what's needed to get your heart racing, your palms sweaty, your fear of failure alarm ringing.

If you're not sweating, you're not stretching. If you're not stretching, you're not feeling discomfort, and you're not feeling discomfort, your goal is not lofty.

Authors James Collins and Jerry Porras described a very lofty goal concept in their 1994 book, Built to Last: Successful Habits of Visionary Companies. In that book, they coined the term BHAG, which stands for Big Hairy Audacious Goal. The term has lived on to inspire a number of dot-com company founders during the development of their vision statements and missions. If a BHAG doesn't make you sweat, then nothing will.

Celebrate Milestones

The goals that make your heart race, the ones that you don't know if they're attainable, will become attainable when you can check some boxes off "complete" along the way. Set milestones are really just smaller goals that make up bigger ones. We all know the saying, "Success breeds success." I really like this saying because it's so true. Nothing makes us feel more accomplished than accomplishing something.

I don't know about you, but I celebrate every accomplishment, no matter how small. If I change a lightbulb, I celebrate it. When I unload the dishwasher and put every last piece of cutlery, every glass and every dish away, I celebrate. If I change the filter in the air conditioner or fill my car with a full tank of gas, I celebrate. We all do. Each chore done gets us that much closer to being able to relax and feel accomplished.

Setting, meeting, and celebrating milestones are increasingly important for goals that will undoubtedly take quite a bit of time, and effort, to achieve. If your goal is to get a four-year degree and you haven't attended your first class yet, you should put in place a great many milestones, beginning with attendance of your first class, completion of your first week, your first month, your first semester, your first year, each following year and graduation - at the very least! Milestones don't cost you anything - unless you're planning to celebrate lavishly. The more the merrier. If you want to consider each individual class you attend to be a milestone, who could argue with you?

Of course, this is coming from the guy who celebrates screwing in a new lightbulb.

Goal Creativity

There's more to goal creativity than goal creation. It's about being creative in your goal creating, or goal setting, process. These are your goals. Take ownership and get funky with them. Maybe you'd like to combine two goals to make them stickier, more fun or more meaningful for you. For example, in the next 12 months I'm going to lose 20 pounds and run a Half Marathon at Disney World. Why combine the two? Are you thinking that I'm robbing myself of completing two goals and only getting the opportunity for one? I see it differently, the two are combined for me. Don't get me wrong, when I lose 20 pounds and it's still three months before the next Disney Half Marathon, I'm celebrating. It's a milestone. But, I'm the type of person who believes less is more. I'd rather have two meaningful events tied together. Do you have any idea how much better I'm going to run when I'm carrying 20 pounds less? My knees know the answer to this question.

Sometimes the more disjointed they are, the better. Maybe they balance themselves out - one is just for fun and one is really serious. Here's an example: Next year I'm going to see a concert at Red Rocks in Amphitheater and land a new job that pays $10,000 or more annually than my current job. One is rather ambitious and makes me sweat. The other sounds like a lot of fun and once I land my new job, I can rationalize planning a trip to Colorado, to see some music in a remarkable setting.

These are your goals. Create them in a way that inspires you. Create them in a way that motivates you, of course, but also create them in a way that makes you smile, maybe even laugh.

Who says that goals need to be so serious? Goals just need to be useful.

Your Goal Plan Can't Wait

You wouldn't take your newborn baby home from the hospital and start thinking about all the things you need to properly clothe, feed and care for him. The same is true for your brand new seven-pound ten-ounce goal. You want this goal to grow healthy and strong, so your plan can't wait.

In all seriousness, too often we make a goal and feel like our job is done. As if the excitement that we feel about committing to a new goal will sustain us and keep us motivated for the long haul. We know from experience that the excitement fades when the real work starts. Whether the real work means studying, making good food choices, waking up earlier, going to sleep earlier or making any other number of sacrifices our new goal requires.

Game planning for success is a no-brainer. *Here's a secret most people overlook; complete the game plan while drawing from the excitement that accompanies the initial commitment to this fantastic new goal.* It's normal to want to sit and savor the excitement of establishing a new goal - and not wanting to dampen that excitement drafting a road map for how to achieve it. That said, be motivated by knowing that the goal on its own is like a flower that's been pulled from the ground. Sure, it looks pretty, but days from now there will be petals on the counter and the flower's best days are surely behind it.

Working your plan is like growing the flowering plant in rich soil. Water it with guidelines, give it the sunshine of structured actions to help it grow, and nurture it with every tool you can build into that keeps you motivated. This whole book is about how discipline = power. The amazing thing that bears repeating, or being said in different ways, is that the right structure and planning gives us power to have the discipline we seek. Like most things in life, it's cyclical.

The Future State

Ask someone who works at a high paid consulting firm, like McKinsey & Company, or The Boston Consulting, and they'll tell you that they spend a lot of time living in the future. Big consulting companies are usually brought in to help companies that are merging with, or acquiring, another company. As you can imagine, such time of transition can lead to a lot of difficult decisions to be made. If it's a merger, which company's policies trump the others when there's a disagreement about process or procedure? Which officers and members of leadership stay, and which are let go, when there is duplication that leads to inefficiency? No wonder the people who work for these consulting companies live in the future state, anything sounds better than dealing with the two simple questions raised above!

The talented people who work for big consulting companies don't just live in the future out of convenience. They are brought in to build the future. So, like us when we set goals, they create the structure needed to get there. It works. But, before they can even begin setting structure and creating a road map, they need buy-in from the people who will be at the helm of leadership in the newly formed entity. To get buy-in they need to paint the picture of where the newly reorganized company will be living once things are ironed out. So, they do that. They propose a future state, and once agreed upon, they can reverse engineer the solutions.

•

When you set a goal, of course you want to achieve it, and you have your eyes on the prize of what achieving that goal will do for you. But do you really believe it's going to happen or are you just okay with the fact that even if you get halfway there, you are better off than where you stand today, so let's just get to it? The problem with this kind of thinking is that you are not "all in."

One of my favorite sayings is "Good enough usually isn't." I think it's been said for so long, by so many people that it's difficult to attribute it to whoever said it first. But, I think about it often, especially when I know that I'm in the middle of a project that I'm tempted to finish expeditiously, but what it needs is for me to devote as much time as is needed to get it right. Well, when you're not "all in" on achieving your goal, you are talking yourself into contentment with a "good enough" option - and you're too good for that!

So, here you are reading a book about how to solidly grasp discipline for its power that leads to successful self-control and goal achievement - and you're being told to live in the future? When it comes to game-planning, we must first live in the future so that we can *really* get our own buy-in. Do some very strong daydreaming. See, feel, smell, taste, and hear what it's like to have fully achieved your new goal. If you can't do this, it will be awfully hard to stay disciplined and committed because a part of you simply doesn't believe it's going to happen. Grant yourself the right to dream. Not always, but just when it comes to fully understanding your goals.

Chapter 6: Deflating Obstacles

> "We choose to go to the moon in this decade and do other things, not because they are easy, but because they are hard, because that goal will serve to organize and measure the best of our energies and skills."
> – John F. Kennedy

As we pursue our goals, and use the power of discipline, we are bound to come upon obstacles that will make it difficult to persevere. Like they say in business, "if it were easy, everyone would do it." As I brought up in earlier chapters, we need to be prepared for the tough times, for times where motivation is hard to come by because those times will surely show up. Fear will show up, fatigue will show up, doubt will show up, and all their negative friends too. If we are ready for them, we can easily defeat them. And each time we defeat our obstacles, we deflate them too. They become smaller and weaker, and the next time we see them, defeating them is even easier.

Life Gets in the Way

There's one person you know who is going to put obstacles more than anyone else. Go have a look in the mirror if you want to see him. He's going to look you in the eye and tell you that this goal is too big, and worse yet, he's going to give you every excuse to give up. The good news is that you know this saboteur. You know how he thinks, you know his tricks, you more than anyone else can be ready and have the discipline to win those arguments. This is why we game-plan. Of course, life gets in the way. You know that and that's why this particular obstacle is old and tired - don't let this one trick you into getting off track.

Yes, someone is going to get sick. Maybe it will be you or someone who depends on you, but that's not an excuse to give up on your goal, to put discipline aside and take the easy way out. That's not who you are and that's not what you're about. This isn't just about being tough enough to tough it out. It's about being smart enough to create alternate strategies when your boat engine dies while you're out at sea. You're creative enough to be resourceful, always. You know that if your car breaks down, you have public transportation or other means to keep on track with your commitments.

This type of resilience does feel like toughness sometimes, and it is, but other times, it's pure intelligence that gets you by. I point this out because some people don't see themselves as tough enough, and they think they'll give up if the going gets rough. However, these same people may see themselves as smart, so there's that angle. If you don't see yourself as tough or smart, I'm just going to have to disagree and not just because you're reading my book. However, let's start there, anyone who's focused on discipline knows that they have the toughness, or the smarts, to increase their discipline quotient.

Most people have a level of toughness and intelligence that's more than sufficient to become successful at anything. It's been proven time and again - that desire trumps raw talent. This is especially true in today's world because of the democratization of informational resources. The internet has indeed taken away much of the power that was granted to those with the means to get a higher education. Regarding toughness, I've yet to know anyone who didn't have a fair amount of it. I've met shy introverts who the outside world would assume were meek, who are anything but. I've also met as many bold extroverts, who look and act tough, but have not one bit of toughness beyond the introverts just mentioned.

Using Role Models

Role models are a funny thing. I don't think most children are cognitive of the fact that they are influenced by them, and adults typically don't see role models as pertinent in our lives because we think of ourselves as fully formed. The poor role models. They are worthy and yet no one is acknowledging them. I, for one, love role models. I see them as people who have characteristics that I admire - and I have different role models for different parts of my own development. When I'm aspiring to be tough, I think of Clint Eastwood, especially the version of him acting out characters in films during the 70s and 80s. Clint is unshakeable regardless of the challenge. If I'm seeking to be inspired by a great thinker, I draw upon the writing of Seth Godin, whose books and blog posts are focused, powerful and wise. When I seek to be kinder and more compassionate, I think about my father and our dinner table conversations that included insights about the value of having empathy for what others experience.

Role models don't have to be good to be influential. As much as we can learn from positive role models who have qualities and characteristics we wish to emulate, we can be positively motivated by negative role models. These would be the people we know, or have known, who embody poor characteristics that motivate us to be very different from them. We've all had run-ins with the teacher, the boss, the friend, the enemy, the neighbor, the waiter who had an assortment of negative qualities. We can draw on poor interactions we've had with bad role models and learn from them. What are the qualities we dislike enough that are carved in our minds thanks to bad, troubling or unhealthy experiences we've had.

Negative role models are typically people who have been anywhere from unkind or aloof to downright mean and nasty. These people have had negative influences on us or someone we care about. Just thinking about certain ones can make your blood boil. That's when you know you have a good negative role model to consider - you are motivated to be very different from them. These exemplary poor role models usually have a mix of bad qualities, some more pronounced than others. We know these people to act in ways that are dishonest, cruel, lazy, rude, impatient, and so on. While it's typically healthier for our mental wellbeing to gain motivation from emulating good role models, it's good to know that when thoughts of people who have been bad to us come to mind, we can take away something positive from what we've learned from them. And when it comes to motivation, it's best that we use every tool possible.

There are a great many high achievers who will tell you that their supreme motivation is to prove wrong the teacher, the coach, the relative, or the friend who told them they couldn't do something. When it comes to obstacles that need deflating, we should consider who the people are that have the potential to create obstacles that derail us.

Obstacle Builders

The negative role models I described above are easy to identify, at least in hindsight. It's nice to know that we can draw benefits from what we learn through those difficult interactions. When it comes to chasing our dreams, achieving our goals, staying disciplined and focused, there are other people we need to consider who can derail us. It may take more work to identify the obstacle builders in our lives because they come in all forms. Unlike the negative role models who we avoid, the obstacle builders are those who we actively engage with in our lives currently. They're not mean spirited, but they have their own goals, their own motivations and their own set of priorities.

The people in our lives who present us with obstacles often do so unknowingly. If your goal is to lose weight and one tactic is to abstain from eating dessert, you certainly can't blame the birthday girl for having cake at the party. Of course, this type of obstacle is one we've game planned for and expected. As is always the case when it comes to commitments and focus, it's the ones we don't expect that provide the biggest challenges. Our number one priority to be true to ourselves, to have the discipline and the power to always be saying yes to walking the path we've chosen.

Just as it's our job to deflate the obstacles that try and stand in our way, it's also our challenge to properly navigate the obstacle builders in our lives. When meeting a goal means getting up for a run at six in the morning, it may be best to avoid the friend who wants you to accompany them to the bar this evening. The bar is an obstacle that needs deflating, and the friend may be one too. Remember, it's not about saying no, it's about saying yes. As we discuss in the next chapter, all we can control is our intention, not how others interpret our actions. A good friend will be happy for you that you have the discipline to say "no" to the bar because you're saying yes to your early morning run. Even if your friend is disappointed, and even if he's not happy for you because of it, he's impressed.

Obstacle Deflating Mindset

Obstacle deflation is a cause for celebration. Anticipating an obstacle and properly avoiding it too. Never miss a chance to build your self-esteem. Too often we wait for someone to lend us a compliment in order to be congratulated. The truth of the matter is that even when we get a compliment, it only lands squarely and makes us feel good if we believe we've earned it. When a six-year-old tells you that you're smart because you rattle off the Jeopardy answer "What is Providence?" as the correct question to answer "The capital of Rhode Island." You may feel a little smart, but you also know that this young child has no idea how badly you'll struggle to get one of the questions correct when the show moves on to the more challenging next round. The same can be true when you're told how strong you are because you can open a jar of pickles - though in all fairness - with some pickle jars that truly is a significant accomplishment. The point being that the most important critic you need to please is you.

Just remember that successfully handling obstacles so that you're not derailed is as important as anything else you can do to move toward goal achievement. Celebrate the smarts it takes to outsmart the obstacle setters and inflators. See every obstacle as an opportunity to show your strength, your determination, and your discipline. Each obstacle you conquer makes you stronger and places you that much closer to goal achievement.

Chapter 7: Intention and Attention

"Let the power of intention lead the way."
— Sharon Salzberg

Sometimes intention is all we have. Life gets noisy and life gets confusing from time to time. When you're feeling introspective, it's normal to ask yourself from time to time, "I wonder how I come off to people? I wonder what they think of me? Have I offended someone? Am I acting selfishly, and if I am, is that a good thing or a bad thing? So, you see, with so many unanswered questions and so many unanswerable questions in life, sometimes all we can do is turn to our intentions for clarity.

Intentions Don't Lie

I love intentions because they serve as our north star. We can trust our intentions because they are true - they are what they are. If I say something in jest and you take offense to it, I may feel bad about that. Of course, I have to ask myself some questions because I genuinely care about your feelings.

I ask the following to gauge my responsibility for hurting your feelings:

- Is my joke off color: is it insensitive?
- Is it my delivery, did I say it the wrong way?
- Should I not tell that joke?

I also ask these questions to myself to gauge your responsibility:
- Are you overly sensitive to this type of content?
- Are you in a vulnerable state because of something affecting you?
- Is your sense of humor off?

Now, to be clear, I realize that I may never know the answer to any of these questions for various reasons. One of those reasons being that I'll infuriate you if I ask the second set of questions, which move along the plane that my joke is perfectly fine and you are being oversensitive, or humorless. That's not going to repair our friendship.

I'll also more likely than not fail at getting answers to the first set of questions as well - at least not based on any solid evidence. That's okay thanks to our hero of the day: intention.

What I can know without a doubt is my intention. If my intention in telling you the joke was to make you laugh, lighten your load and bring joy into your life, I can live with my decision to tell it. If my intention was to hurt you, then I'm a jerk, and I succeeded. Because I have some level of confidence about myself and how I operate, I'm going to go with, "I'm a good guy, but my joke failed to produce its desired effect."

This example is a tough one to be totally okay with. My intentions don't absolve me from wrongdoing. I owe you an apology because my joke hurt your feelings. The truth is my good intentions didn't spare you the hurt. If I'm truly a well-intentioned person, I care about that.

My apology to you will include an explanation about my intent, and that may help. It may leave you feeling like I made a bad decision to tell the joke, but I'm not a bad person. Everyone makes mistakes, right?

I'm grateful to know that when in doubt, I can turn to my intentions and know 100% what's in my heart. I can question you about your intentions and gain quite a bit of clarity about who you are as a person, what you care about, and how you move through the world.

Power of Attention

It's hard to overestimate the importance of our attention. When I think about attention, my mind immediately turns to thought of gratitude because of the awesome power that accompanies our ability to have command over our attention. Don't get me wrong, having this command is no small feat, and we all suffer lapses from time to time. Without control over our attention, the probability that we will be successful at anything is greatly diminished. The focus required to achieve our goals requires that we are disciplined enough to focus our attention where it does us the most good.

Sure, it sounds simple enough to maintain control over this incredibly valuable commodity we own, but sure enough, it's not simple. it's also not easy, and without the serious effort to exert control, attention to the things that matter to us most is incredibly hard to maintain. It's not because our mind is soft, it's really a matter of how big the challenge is to juggle so many obligations that are important to us. It's for this reason that paying attention to our priorities offers the best chance we have for paying attention to the things that matter most. Once again, we see that circular logic is at play. In other words, we need to pay attention to how we pay attention. If that sounds confusing, reread it, it's rather important and will make sense upon a second read if it didn't register as sound advice the first time.

The Attention Economy

So valuable is our attention that marketing professionals have coined the term "attention economy" to ascribe the value of capturing and holding attention. Social media platforms like, Google, Facebook, and Twitter, live on the attention economy. Our attention is so valuable to digital companies that they're willing to operate at a loss, sometimes for years on end, while they grow their audience because they know that if they have our attention, they'll figure out pretty quickly how to monetize that achievement.

This was true before the internet and social media became so good at garnering our attention. Television and radio stations work on a similar advertising driven model. If they assemble entertaining content that commands our attention, they can sell access to our attention to advertisers. When we break it down like this it becomes crystal clear that our attention has immense value. The billion-dollar question is, "Are we being careful enough with what we do with our attention?" If we are truly entertained, maybe we're okay with seeing commercial content so that someone can pay the entertainment bill.

Another answer to the question of where we put our attention is, "Oh my gosh. I've really not given enough thought into where I allow my attention to drift from time to time. Maybe some of the things I allow to distract me are benefiting others, but not me." If you have this type of awakening, do not allow yourself to become too alarmed. Sunk costs with regard to your attention are not the issue. The real issue is determining what steps to take to make sure that you benefit most from the choices concerning your attention. To be clear-minded about the real value of attention and the power you wield - that's what matters most!

May I Have Your Attention?

With a newfound respect for the value of your attention, you may think twice about who requests your attention, how they do it, and how you react. If we are in a public space that's equipped with a microphone and speaker system, we may not be too surprised when we hear over the loudspeaker "May I have your attention, please?" When this happens in a supermarket, our ears perk up, but we realize it may just be an announcement that the deli department has a great sale going on for Taylor ham by the slice. But it also may be something more serious, ranging from news about the license plate for a car with light left on, to something even more serious, like a missing child. Yes, they can have our attention, what choice do we have?

Marketers are not so forthcoming as to announce their intention to get your attention. They are, however, equally disruptive, and often more so due to the stealth nature of certain tactics. Now, I'm not bashing marketers or marketing, it's a noble profession when done with respect for the consumer. Yet, we all know that we are living in an age where the internet has opened new channels for marketers to connect with us, and to get our attention, often without asking.

Think about how hard some companies work to get our attention and it can make your head spring. In some instances, it's truly alarming. If you are one of the 2.6 billion Facebook users on the planet, you know full well how much that platform wants your attention. You would think that they would have enough of a hook for us to show up periodically that the company should be satisfied. But we know that's not true. They don't sit back satisfied and wait for us to show up. They send you an email that teases you - telling you that your friend, uncle, business partner, or mother has posted something new that you should check out. The Facebook marketing team knows what they've just done to you. They've taken their best shot at taking your attention away from your other emails, to get you to visit the Facebook platform and see what's going on.

When Facebook interrupts your perusal of emails with this, "Jenny A. just posted an update ..." they know that you likely can't resist because while Cousin Jenny *may* just be posting another image of her incredibly cute dog, she also might be posting an update about her mom's recovery from illness - and what kind of person are you if you don't keep up with how Aunt Nancy is healing? Yes, you are being manipulated. You may not mind, or you may dislike it, but it is what it is. Unless you feel strongly enough about it and do something about it. That something may range from a change of settings so that you don't get these types of emails from Facebook - to simply making a decision that you'll not read or react to these emails because you have other places where you'd like to keep your attention focused.

A couple more things about Facebook and Cousin Jenny. First of all, neither of them is acting maliciously, but your attention is valuable, it is something you own, and it's something that you can decide how to manage. You also can decide to do so without feeling guilty, and that speaks to your *intention*. The other thing to mention about the size of the attention theft Facebook commits with this tactic is based on size of theft. Facebook marketing professionals know that not only does our attention go to Cousin Jenny's post, but while we're on the platform we are also exposed to the posts of others in our "news feed." As you check to see what Jenny posted you can't help but see that your best friend from high school became an uncle, and that your oversharing friend, Charlie, is once again treating himself to a steak dinner.

Hands Off My Attention

Yes, the battle for your attention is in full force. You didn't choose this battle, but you are most certainly in it. As you can see, some of the themes we've covered thus far are applicable to the issue of attention. Those who take our attention away from goal-oriented focus are putting up obstacles. The game plan we've spoken about is more important than ever when we consider that our best strategy to win the attention battle is to have a strategy, to be prepared, so that we can be vigilant. Marketers grab us by surprise. It's a real component of the tactics they use to disrupt the flow of where our attention was heading before their content showed up.

"Disrupt" is a marketing term used often. In the case of start-up companies like Uber and Ebay, disruption is certainly accurate in describing their impact, right? After all, Uber's entry into the transportation market not only disrupted the taxicab industry, it downright upended it. The same can be said of Ebay, the online marketplace that killed the revenue that newspapers used to charge people to list items they were seeking to sell. The poor newspaper industry lost similar advertising revenues due to disruption from digital startups in the real estate, auto sales and help wanted industries too. As you can see, disruption can have costly consequences.

When it comes to your attention, it's up to you to not be disrupted. It's a matter of focus, right? This is where the power of discipline comes in handy. You own the power to ignore advertisements, not matter how enticing, when you are on a mission to accomplish your goals and time is of the essence. The time your attention is hijacked is time you can't get back. Be vigilant with your time-management skills. Apply the power of discipline to impose your will over that of the marketers and brands they represent. Be prepared for the sneak attacks we've seen before, the emails that tease, the "timely offers" that demand your attention now. Stay focused because the timely offers will be there again tomorrow (sorry marketers, but you know it's true).

The emails that tease you and make play off of your FOMO (Fear Of Missing Out) can be ignored if you're committed to staying true to your own set of priorities - not someone else's.

Acting with Intention

Intention is the best friend your attention could ask for. Good intentions allow us to combat FOMO and the fear of missing an update about Aunt Nancy's recovery from Cousin Jenny. Either you'll miss it and learn about it from someone else at another time, or you won't, but your intentions are good if your intention is to stay true to reaching a goal. Use your well-intentioned motivations as a suit of armor. No one who cares about you has the right to make you feel bad about being disciplined and staying true to your priorities. These are admirable characteristics. Allow these healthy choices to be anchored by good intentions. When our intentions are good, we don't owe apologies - to others or ourselves. The same is not true when our intentions are poor, or when we simply wander without the guiding star of intention.

When you commit to a goal, be sure to include intention front and center in your game plan for goal achievement. Better yet, take some time to think about where you'll need to place your attention. Tie the two together to ensure that you are intentional about your attention. Being intentional about where we put our attention has the wonderful byproduct of excluding where we won't put our attention. Realize that when you focus on your attention, and follow your intention, you won't be perfect. You'll forget. You'll make mistakes. You'll get sucked into Facebook, or Instagram, or Twitter or another social media platform when your intention isn't to do so. At the point you realize it, you can do what the talented mindfulness practitioners do. Start over. Simply begin again. It's powerful and a healthy habit - far better than beating yourself up for it - or saying something along the lines of "I'm not good at this." You're human. You are good at it. You're just not perfect.

Chapter 8: Using the Power of Discipline

> "Discipline is the bridge between goals and accomplishment"
>
> – Jim Rohn

Up to this point, we've spent a fair amount of time speaking about goals, motivations, focus and any number of things that rely on discipline for their success. It's easy to understand how, without discipline, we are powerless to achieve our goals. When we look at goal achievement on a cellular level, we discover that discipline lies at the nucleus. Simply stated, it's discipline that provides us with the power to make good decisions. Discipline is what helps us say no to unhealthy choices and yes to solutions that provide meaningful benefits. Of course, what you may find confusing is this question "if discipline is so simple to understand and so helpful for building the life we want, why don't we use it all the time?" The most honest answer I can provide is that we're human and being disciplined all the time is a perfectionist idea that's not achievable.

A Powerful Perspective

As you seek to master self-control and use the power of discipline to build better habits, it's helpful to keep in mind that the first goal is improvement. If you strive to become a masterful martial artist, you must first earn belts of various colors before you ascend the black belt levels of achievement. The reason I bring up perspective is not to derail your focus from the pinnacle of your discipline goal, but to help you realize that you may seek progress as a goal rather than something more absolute.

The best way to harness the power of discipline is to have a healthy relationship with discipline, something we touched upon earlier. Discipline provides us with the fuel to achieve many things, but to be disciplined our motivations and focus must align. I say "celebrate every achievement" because it takes determination to choose discipline and that determination needs fuel of its own.

The Power to Create Good Habits

Clinical studies have provided conflicting data regarding the number of days it takes to build a good habit. It's easy to understand why when you consider how many different factors come into play depending on what type of habit we're considering, not to mention the fact that people are unique. For years, motivational experts touted 30 days as the amount of time it should take to create a new habit. More recently, that number was put squarely at 21 days, and even more recently, studies have squashed the 21-day theory as an unfounded myth and some suggest that it may be more than 60 days to establish.

Let's not be dissuaded by unprovable theories and realize that it doesn't really matter. If I'm trying to create a good habit to run five or more days a week every week, that realization of whether or not I've created a habit is solely up to me to decide. Have I established the habit when I've done it three weeks in a row, five weeks in row, 12 weeks? Perhaps I've established the habit when I do it x number of weeks in a row and then feel withdrawal symptoms the first week when I don't run five or more times. That sounds about right, doesn't it; that proof of a habit is suffering withdrawal upon ceasing to do it? The bottom line is how we define it is based upon our own subjective feelings concerning when we believe we are on solid footing with regard to being over the hurdle of needing to call on discipline to accomplish something.

This brings us to the value of a good habit. A good habit means we are in a rhythm and we can use less discipline power to keep showing up for ourselves. Ideally, this would allow us to point our discipline power toward the next goal, this one being fully accomplished and all. Yet, if you've lived long enough and had the privilege to develop habits, both good and bad, you know that while the bad habits are tough to break, the good habits are easy to end without effort. Bad habits are typically those that are driven by our subconscious and good habits most often require more use of our conscious mind. This is especially true when we consider the development of these habits.

It is comforting to know that we can build a good habit, and that in doing so, the effort required is reduced as we move along. This is true with most things, that the most difficult steps are the initial steps, usually with the first taking significantly more effort than those that follow. If we look at certain good habits we want to establish, we'll see that there are those where the first step is hardest because it includes stepping into the unknown, and others where the first step is less difficult to take because we are pumped up with adrenaline, something that we know will likely diminish in the subsequent steps.

If I'm building a good habit of going to the gym to workout four times a week, the first time I do it may be relatively easy because I'm following through on a newly made commitment and my goal benefits are top of mind. Yet, if I've joined a new gym that I've never visited before, this is a significantly harder first step to take because of my fear of the unknown. The effort to go to this new gym includes directing some of my energy to quelling my mind, with my questions of "will it be crowded at the time I'm going?" and "What will the vibe be like in this new gym - judgmental, supportive, something else?"

If the good habit I'm seeking to create is to eat healthier and skip eating dessert until I hit my ideal weight, the first meal I approach may be the easiest, as I'm excited by my new commitment. As time goes on, if I feel deprived, rather than becoming a healthy habit that's easy to follow, it may be tougher to feel increasingly denied. The energy I'll need to remain disciplined about building this habit will likely increase as time goes on, not diminish. On the other hand, if this habit forms the way I hope, my desire for dessert may fade over time, and therefore require less energy for a disciplined approach.

The bottom line is that the amount of energy needed to use our power of discipline to establish a good habit depends on the various factors involved in the actions to be taken.

Discipline for Career Success

One place where the power of discipline is clear to discern is in the workplace. I don't say this because of the obvious things we typically think of, like career advancement. I say it because regardless of your opportunities for advancement - many of which may be beyond your control - the workplace is a structured environment with measuring sticks we can use to grade our own performance. Realize the importance of grading your own work. When you have the power of discipline, there's no need to give your power away to anyone else - whether it's a manager, boss. or any other person holding an appointed position. You have the power to decide when you are successful. Your definition of success may differ from that belonging to others in your workplace. Success is not something that someone can bestow upon you, it's a quality that only matters when you can claim it, when you feel it, when it's undeniably yours.

Discipline in the workplace goes well beyond showing up on time, or early and leaving late. Your workplace discipline is important when it's aligned with your workplace goals and complying with the actions you deem relevant to reaching those goals. Let's be clear about this: If your place of employment has a leadership team that does not, for any reason, earn your respect, it's of little consequence whether or not they are impressed with your work ethic and your discipline. If you're fortunate to be employed by a company with a leadership team overseeing your work for whom you do have respect, there's something to be gained by impressing those leaders with your application of discipline in the workplace, but once again, it pales when compared to your own assessment.

Too often, employees focus their energies solely on impressing leadership staff. Any leadership team member worthy of concern will likely care more about what you do to support your peers and contribute to the company's success on any level. The power of discipline empowers you to maintain focus, do your best work and contribute to high quality outcomes. Smart business leaders understand that talent comes and goes - rarely is talent valued above effort. When you are disciplined in your approach to work, a strong effort comes easily. Discipline means you're the one who follows through; it's you who is counted on because you need only be asked to do something once; and best of all, it's you who inspires others.

Discipline for Powerful Leadership

Great leaders don't lean on discipline in order to lead, but their discipline is a leadership quality that allows them to lead. I'm not referring merely to the easy to spot acts of discipline like showing up early, staying late or enforcing workplace guidelines. The discipline that creates powerful leadership is largely related to that which supports consistency. More than anything else, in the workplace we seek leaders who are consistent about what they believe, what they preach, what they expect and what they bring to the table.

Oftentimes, it's leaders who lack these discipline-driven qualities who obviate the importance of such characteristics. The would-be leaders who are inconsistent, irrational, unreasonable - these failing leaders make us yearn for solid footing. When a leader with discipline emerges in a workplace where a failing leader is present, it's without effort and often without intent that the individual with leadership qualities usurps power. It's the dependable leader who people follow, regardless of their rank or status.

Leaders who are disciplined in their approach are magnetic. So strong is their foundation that it strengthens those around them. In the presence of a disciplined leader, others too can lead. In fact, disciplined leaders are more likely to deputize others because they realize the value of leadership and they know that real leadership is renewable energy. The more it's shared, the more of it there is to go around. Disciplined leaders believe in the power of the abundance theory over any theory of scarcity.

The disciplined leader is charitable and generous. So too is the disciplined leader compassionate, understanding that the discipline that's evident in her approach to leadership is an attractive quality sought by many - and those who are not *yet* capable of it are not to be overlooked, pitied or treated with disdain. Discipline lives on a spectrum. Everyone has it to varying degrees and with encouragement, anyone can become more disciplined. Hence the need for disciplined leadership.

The Power of Discipline is Contagious

Just as we speak of the magnetism of disciplined leadership, the quality can be equally admired and respected when revealed in anyone, and within any organization. Too often, organizations seek to demand discipline without building the structure needed to support it - whether it's due to a vacuum in leadership or a culture that is misaligned. Conversely, discipline can be the cornerstone of culture when it's defined and promoted in an attractive light.

Start-up companies are often big on touting a corporate culture that reciprocates the sacrifices that employees make to contribute wholeheartedly to the company's success. These companies seek to gain loyalty by demonstrating their commitment to building a culture that values a balanced lifestyle. Ironically, the types of amenities that have become synonymous with these companies - perks like massages, free snacks and meals, napping pods, ping-pong and happy hours - can also be seen as offerings to maximize time spent productively working. This can be a funny way of promoting balance between work and lifestyle.

I'm not putting down start-up culture in the companies, like Google and Facebook, who are known to offer the types of perks I've mentioned. To their credit, they use such perks to attract employees who want these types of features available at work, and perhaps for some ambitious staff, the potential to enjoy their time at work offsets any real need to balance their time at work with time spent at home. The value that's being created is that it does contribute to a unique culture and one that rewards workplace discipline.

The interesting thing about the contagious nature of discipline is that it can be spontaneous. In my experience, I've witnessed discipline contagion more often when it's not planned or created purposefully, at least in the workplace. Discipline that takes shape and transfers from one individual to the next - often spurred on by actions that are noticeable and admirable - is the type of discipline that can propel an organization to a level of success unanticipated.

The Power of Discipline for Learning

More often than not, we look to discipline to fuel changes in life that seem to be insurmountable without it. Students learn early on that without discipline, academic achievement is unlikely. Sure, there's always the appearance that for some people, academic achievement comes easy and the discipline to study is not even summoned. Yet, for others - in fact, the majority of us - academic achievement is all but impossible without the discipline required for study. When we think about it more closely, what is learning, but a constant state of change. It's remarkable when you consider that as human beings we are always learning - which means that we are always changing.

What's fascinating about the human condition, and the mind in particular, is that learning opportunities are ubiquitous. How much we learn and the rate at which we learn is largely determined by our discipline to point our attention in direction rather than another. Think about something as simple as a commute to work. Whether you drive, take a train or a bus, the choice of where to put your attention is yours, and yet regardless of where you focus it, learning opportunities abound. If you listen to music on the radio, you're bound to hear a new song, and that's a learning event. Even if you hear a song you've heard before, the meaning of a particular lyric may register with you in a way it never did before. In that moment, learning and change occur.

What if on that same commute you choose to listen to a recorded book or podcast. In doing so you have an opportunity to learn at a higher rate. Depending on your intent and your choices, that learning may be a part of your disciplined approach to learning. Think for a moment at what happens each time you consume a news program, and the accelerated rate of change that's occurring in your mind. Isn't every unique newscast a learning opportunity? If so, is it done mindfully, as a discipline you keep to grow your knowledge base about current events, about the world around you? This application of disciplined learning may feel like a stretch from how we typically think of the concept, but it really shows how closely discipline and attention are related. It also reminds us that discipline covers a broad range. Yet discipline always presents us the power to change, and learning is most certainly the way we change most often.

The true power of discipline for learning is tied to the way that what we learn affects how we think. How we think affects what we do and what we do affects what we become. If you like self-help books, you may have come across this idea before. I know from my readings that I've seen Zig Ziglar use this reference a number of times. That said, Zig doesn't own this piece of knowledge, which in fact is the basis for what 's taught in the study of cognitive psychology.

Staying with this theme - that what we learn affects who we become - how much more mindful should we be about what we listen to, and who we choose to listen to. With regard to listening to, or watching, daily news reports there's a longstanding concern shared by many that because bad news is covered more than good news, the broadcasts lead to a mindset of pessimism. We can debate this forever; whether the news media's coverage of bad news is depressing, or whether it's an accurate coverage of what is newsworthy - and therefore is simply what we should know about the world around us. That said, it's our own responsibility to decide for ourselves whether we should be disciplined to point our attention in the direction of media news or away from it.

If you choose to use your discipline to avoid the news media for any given reason, you're doing something healthy because you're flexing your discipline muscles. Making such a choice need not be an absolute. It may be part of a decision you make to draw your attention elsewhere for a period of time. You may make a choice like this because you're simply busy, or you may make a decision to avoid broadcast news as part of an experiment, to see if you feel differently. How powerful does that make you feel? Understanding that you can change your emotional state by changing what you allow to stimulate your brain.

It all comes back to learning and choices. Is it a paradigm shift for you to realize that you are *always* learning? How many new things do you think you learn each day? It seems reasonable that if you listen to a half hour news program you may learn 15 new things. Our perspective is such that we don't typically think of little things as learning. However, if you hear that tonight's weather is going down 30 degrees from where it was in the middle of the day, that's something you've learned. It certainly is relatively inconsequential. It's not even a piece of learning that you would ever apply again, as it's use is that short term. If you watch a newscast and hear a political reporter relay a piece of history that you think is really interesting, you may learn of a story that sticks with you for the rest of your life.

Here's an example of a story I heard relayed by a political historian on a news station recently that I found interesting. The historian told what I believe to be a well-known story about the connection the American public felt for former president Franklin Delano Roosevelt. The story describes a tribute paid to the former president as a part of his funeral procession included his body traveling by train through a number of small towns. People lined up along the tracks just to see the funeral train pass by, as it contained the body of FDR. A reporter covering the event as the train passed by in Warm Springs, GA saw an onlooker crying and asked that man, "Did you know the president personally?" to which the man replied, "No, but he knew me." I heard this story spoken by that historian a number of months ago and yet, I find it so powerful that I'm confident that it will be indelible in my mind.

Discipline Power for Conquering the Mundane

When we think about the learning process for larger and more important skills, we have to consider how those types of breakthroughs occur - and what motivation gets us there. By there, I mean the moment we go from *not* being able to do it to *being able to do it*. If you've ever learned to play a sport and been taught a new technique, you know what it feels like to try and fail - again and again - sometimes day after day, maybe even week after week - and then suddenly be able to do what you couldn't do before. There are psychologists who debate how this type of learning happens. In one camp they believe that it's a matter of small increments each time you try, and each attempt builds until those small increments stand on each other's shoulders and push you over the edge. The other camp believes that it's not incremental; that each of those attempts is an all-out failure, but your brain is processing - and then it's sudden, not incremental that you go from nothing to all. It could be argued that the latter is just a nuance of the former - that the failures are training your brain for the major shift and those failures aren't really failures, they are incremental builds.

Regardless of how you believe breakthroughs occur, every attempt, every practice that equates to you working the process is often painstaking and what many people consider mundane. The discipline to do the mundane is truly what separates many successful people from their counterparts. As you might expect, they aren't superhuman. Some are super disciplined, but there's a trick. That trick is that they don't think of the mundane as mundane. They bring passion and desire to every practice, every failed attempt. They don't see the failed attempts as failure because they trust the process. You hear coaches and teachers say it often, "Trust the process." When they say it, they may as well be clergy members because they're really saying, "Have faith."

If you spend everyday trying to master a skill that you never have before - learning to play piano for example - whether practice is mundane or an opportunity to pursue a passion is up to you. The lessons are the same, but the approach, the mindset and the motivation are what's different.

It makes you wonder about the people who appear to have natural talent - for music - sports - fine art - are they born with that talent or are they born with more excitement for practicing the mundane and seeing it as something more from the very first step?

The famous story told about Michael Jordan, maybe the greatest basketball player ever to lace up sneakers, is that he was cut from his high school basketball team his sophomore year. Do you mean to tell me that Michael Jordan, one of the most graceful athletes of all time is not a natural talent? His high school coaches didn't see him as one during his sophomore year. How about the power of determination? Did that blow to his ego motivate him? It appears that his competitive nature, which was likely stirred by that perceived failure is what motivated him to attack the mundane, practice his heart out, and come into college athletics looking like "a natural."

One more thought about "the mundane." Every mundane task is a challenge, whether we are excited enough by the larger goal that it feels small - or whether we are feeling unmotivated, in which case the mundane task can feel monumental. It's the times when we feel weakest that we can *lean* on discipline to be sure that we get it done. Discipline gives us that power because we can take the guesswork and the debate out of consideration. The mundane task must be done because we trust the process, and we trust the process because we will not be denied on the road to achieving our goal. The goal, of course, means so very much to us because it represents an opportunity to make good on the promise we've already made to ourselves.

Discipline equals power because it is the framework of success. Without it, there's little we can do to enforce that we will follow through, that we will honor our promises. Discipline holds our feet to the fire - in a really good and supportive way.

Chapter 9: Celebrating Every Step

"The more you praise and celebrate your life, the more there is in life to celebrate."
– Oprah Winfrey

In an earlier chapter I touched upon the importance of celebrating goal achievement at every level. This issue is so critical to success that it deserves a deeper dive. Not because we need to pat ourselves on the back and say good job so that we can take our foot off the gas. It's the opposite. Celebrating every step gives us more power. Power that fuels discipline - and as we know discipline equals power, so we create "the cycle of achievement."

The reason to celebrate every achievement is that without a completed goal potentially goes unnoticed. So, forget about a missed opportunity to enjoy our success, if we miss an opportunity to acknowledge our success, it works against us. The reason for this is that it takes power away from our goal achieving motivation. If on one hand we say create, "let's create goals to help us work our game plan and achieve what we want, so that we can be happy," and then we achieve a goal without even noticing, we've broken the promise of being happy about our achievements.

Maybe this seems nitpicky, too much minutiae or "getting into the weeds" on the issue of celebration, but it's really a risk-reward relationship. When we create a goal - no matter how large or small - we take a risk. Deciding to do something is making a commitment to ourselves.

Making a commitment involves risk. The risk is about what happens if we fail to meet our commitment. Failing hurts us. It hurts our self-esteem and without that, we feel less brave to make the next commitment, set the next goal.

Yin and Yang

In life, we continually see the Yin and the Yang - two forces of balance in the universe. The concept of Yin and Yang stems from ancient Chinese philosophy and focuses on the balance of the dark and light. Surely, you're familiar with the circular image - showing a black shape and white shape taking up space in equal halves of the sphere. This balance is true in the nature of our world, and exists everywhere. Across the planet, it couldn't be more evident than the repetitive presence of night and day. Our own body's need to balance energy between awake and sleep, according to the circadian rhythms that governs it. In fact, even the energy that surrounds is always in balance. Think about how unique it is that we live with the law of conservation of energy, which states that energy remains constant - it *"can neither be created nor destroyed; rather, it can only be transformed or transferred from one form to another."*

The reason to consider yin and yang in the context of celebrating every achievement is because the reasoning is most obvious, most meaningful, when we weigh it against what happens when we don't do it. The light of celebration in respect to the darkness of nonobservance. The power of discipline that is rewarded when we celebrate every step versus the weakening of our power when we fail to celebrate and give way to the darkness of not acknowledging achievement. If this makes you roll your eyes and say, "sounds a bit dramatic for something as insignificant as celebrating every little achievement" then you're choosing to ignore how the power of discipline works at the molecular level.

Is it very necessary to dissect the power and energy of achievement at the molecular level? The reason that the answer is a resounding "yes" is that the power of discipline is elusive for so many reasons. To best understand it, so that we can harness it, we should leave no stone unturned. Every part of this book is intended to make this elusive power stop being so - and we know it's possible because we see it manifested every day. And, thanks to the balance of our universe, we see it dissipate.

If the power of discipline is the light and its absence is the dark, doesn't the balance of our world indicate that we cannot expect to capture the power of discipline in a way that is absolute? That's right. The most disciplined, motivated and accomplished among us don't get to claim absolute power over anything. Remember, the goal is not perfection. The goal is excellence. The best we can do to seize the power of discipline is to understand, call upon it at will, use it as best as possible - and realize that we will have to balance it out with giving our body and mind the rest we deserve. The army drill sergeant may be a master of discipline, but he too sleeps, he too is human, and he too has a lapse in discipline from time to time.

Celebration Is Not the End

Everything in life is framed by our perspective. If you believe that a celebration of achievement is the final act, then it is. Yet, we all know that when one door closes another one opens. Let every celebration of a goal achieved be the launching ceremony for the next one. As long as we are living we are growing, and every goal we accomplish begins our journey to achieve the next. This is not to say that we only look ahead. We do celebrate and take our victory lap. We do stop to smell the roses. When we do so, we are living in the moment, and being present is the healthiest mindset we can have. So, as we celebrate our achievements, we sit at the precipice of completion of one goal and launch of the next. In this moment, we take the energy from one goal and transfer it to the next. Remember, energy is neither created nor destroyed; it's merely transferred.

Here's an interesting question: What if we end an attempt to complete a goal without completing it, can we celebrate a goal we do not complete? The short answer is yes. When we put a goal to rest mindfully, we can celebrate. Celebration is simply a form of acknowledgement. It's positive of course. I mean, you could acknowledge something with a neutral tone and that would not be celebratory. You could also acknowledge something's completion with a negative tone; that certainly would not be a celebration. In ending an attempt to complete a goal with achieving it, maybe there's a good reason, or a great one, for ending our effort when we do.

If I'm training to run a marathon and I have an accident whereby I break a bone in my foot, and the marathon I'm training for is two weeks away, the healthy thing for me to do is to end my efforts toward achieving that goal. Whether I see it as worthy of celebration is up to me. I could perceive it as a negative thing, as a failure. I could view it as neutral, as "stuff happens." I could also see it as an opportunity. "When one door closes …" What choice do you think I make? You've got that right, I celebrate. I have nothing to be remorseful about. I did my best to train for the marathon. I made strides (double entendre intended). And, yes, "stuff happens," but guess what? I just gained two weeks of opportunity to reallocate time I would have spent training and use that energy toward another goal. I could use that time to write my book, to spend more quality time with my family, to learn a new song on the guitar, and about a hundred different things I'd like to pursue.

Optimism Wins

Stop me if you've heard this one. The pessimist sees the glass as half full. The optimist sees it as half empty. The engineer sees the glass as twice as big as it needs to be. Talk about perception being everything, right? When it comes to optimism, there are those who resist it because, while they insist they are not pessimists, they claim to be realists. Let's get this straight, realism and optimism are not at odds with one another. That's a fact. Look up the antonym of optimism and you'll see that it's pessimism. Here's the good news, you can be a realist and an optimist.

The definition of a realist is "a person who accepts a situation as it is and is prepared to deal with it accordingly." Isn't it true that a realist, someone who is prepared to deal with the situation as it is, can take an optimist approach to being "prepared to deal with it accordingly?" I'm certain that these principles can coexist. In the scenario of the marathon and my broken foot, as a realist, I was prepared to not run the race. I too was an optimist in that I discovered so many opportunities to spend time I would have spent training to further my achievement toward another goal that matters to me. I could easily have been pessimistic about what was "real" and dwelled on what the accident prohibited me from doing. I chose to be optimistic and focus on the opportunities.

Optimism is a choice. It's a mindset. So important is it to a healthy and happy frame of mind, you'll find that mental health experts tout it as paramount to one's well-being. Optimism and hope are closely related. The definition of optimism is along the lines of having confidence in the future, or the success of something. Hope, on the other hand, is more about "having faith" that something you want might happen. They are similar in that they are both mindsets that can be chosen, and that make us happier when we choose them. Hope is a common theme among professionals within the field of addiction treatment. Many will attest that addiction so breaks the human spirit that only a mindset of hope can begin to repair it. It's hard to imagine a stronger endorsement than that for the power of mindset.

Optimism and Discipline

As you can see, mindset is so important to capturing the power of discipline that we examine every angle at defining and acquiring the right mindset to create it. Optimism is exactly what we need to become disciplined and to maintain discipline. Without, the pessimistic mindset takes over and tells us things that dissuade us from making good on our promise. The pessimistic part of our brain, when we allow it to take hold, tells us any of the following things are true:

- This doesn't matter
- You will fail
- You failed before; it will happen again
- You're wasting your time
- You should be focused on something else

Conversely, the optimistic mindset tells us that these things are true:
- This really matters
- You will succeed
- You are on a good course
- This is a great investment of your time
- You are growing as a person
- You can't fail
- You should be proud of yourself

You can see how these points illustrate the ways in which pessimism saps our strength, while optimism fuels our desire to achieve. Discipline is starved by pessimism and fortified by optimism. You already know this. You've experienced this in life. You've doubted yourself enough to pass on a chance at something because you didn't know how it would turn out - something that you deserved a chance at - and even a failure at trying would have been more satisfying than sitting it out.

You also know the power of optimism because of the times you took a chance, feeling vulnerable and you got some positive feedback. That positive feedback nurtured you, gave you a jolt of confidence and that jot of confidence turned into an optimistic outlook on taking the next step in that particular journey. That optimistic outlook, which sprouted from that one hit of confidence, even gave you the courage to take a chance on something else you wanted, despite feeling vulnerable.

When it's discipline that you seek; discipline to take the first step, or the next, let optimism be your spark plug. You may be thinking, that would be easy if I were an optimist, but I'm not, I'm a realist (very few people admit to being pessimists). This comes back to what was presented earlier in this chapter - to ability for realism and optimism to coexist. In fact, I'm certain that you're better served being both rather than one or the other. Be a realist. It's unhealthy to be anything else. Be honest with yourself - and that's not always easy. You may know this about yourself, or you may see it in others. Some people have real trouble with the truth. I'm not saying that they are bad or purposefully dishonest; it's just that some people get so good at rationalization that they can rationalize any behavior, and do it by distorting reality, particularly with regard to the future, where facts are simply hard to come by.

The best reason for being a realist is that you can make the best decisions when you are not rationalizing or making giant leaps of faith too often. Being a realist is simply a healthy mindset. It's healthiest when it coexists with being an optimist. As an optimist and a realist, you're saying to yourself "I don't know how this project or this event will play out in the future, but I feel good about it and I'm going to be motivated by my belief that it's more likely going to turn out the way I want it to rather than not." Nowhere is this mindset of optimism untrue or nonrealistic. We obviously don't have control over the future, but we have the right to believe what we want about our chances.

While we have the right to choose our beliefs, if our beliefs are inconsistent from what experience has taught us, then perhaps we do drift away from realism - so it's up to us to hold ourselves accountable for "keeping it real." There are grey areas in life. How do you know if you're being realistic if you're trying to accomplish something new" If there's nothing in your past experience that provides insight into your probability for success, how could you know? You don't. When venturing into the unknown, we owe it to ourselves to make the best educated guess we can make, drawing comparisons to things that we have experienced. That said, as long as failure is not fatal, or even harmful in any significant way, then we can and should be bolder about trying something new. How else do we get experience and knowledge about it?

Celebrating Optimism

Knowing that optimism is the healthiest choice for a mindset that fosters motivation and discipline, the question is how do you maintain our sense of optimism? And if you're not an optimist, how do you change? If you believe the compelling argument made so far, that optimism is not only healthy, it's critical for maintaining discipline, then you have your motivation to want to change, and as life teaches us, if we have the motivation we are much more than halfway there.

Just as we celebrate achievements to harness the power they provide to tackle the next challenge, we can celebrate optimism for what it provides us. Even that second time when you got on the bicycle and were pretty sure it wasn't going to go well, you had just enough optimism to give it a try. If you were one hundred percent sure that you were going to fail, you would not have tried. I referenced the second time you got on the bicycle and not the first for a reason. The first time, you may have had more optimism, been less afraid and less concerned because you didn't know what to expect. It's after that first time didn't go the way you hoped that you needed to dig deeper, and had more reason to quit, that optimism grew in importance.

When you succeeded in riding the bicycle without falling over, you didn't think to yourself, "Thank you optimism for making this possible," but if you had it would have been well placed praise. No worries. You were a kid, optimism wasn't on your mind. Now you're grown up. You have a sense of fear, and a fear of failure, that is quite larger than it was back then. Now, you need every tool in your toolbox to increase your probability for success.

Celebrating optimism begins with acknowledging optimism, what it can do for you and what it has done for you. As a kid, it was okay to give no props to optimism for your bike riding success. Now, however, it's optimism that gives you the courage to send in your resume for a job that you may or may not be most qualified for, or even sufficiently qualified at all. Sometimes we just don't know. Oftentimes, we don't know. We do need to take a leap of faith from time to time. That leap of faith is launched by optimism. If you are a religious person, you may or may not credit optimism for your faith. However, if you first fell in love with faith because you liked the idea of going to heaven or you simply liked the way it made you feel - optimism was at play in either instance, or a third instance if it was the mix of the two - or something altogether different that motivated you. Now you know that you can celebrate optimism for allowing you to choose faith. You can also celebrate optimism for that warm feeling that having faith gives you. It's based on optimism.

As you can see, the power of optimism and the power of discipline go hand in hand. Discipline fails without motivation. Motivation fails without optimism. The more we acknowledge and celebrate the role that optimism plays in producing positive energy, the more we support a healthy and productive mindset. Remember that optimism is that spark plug that initiates your motivational engine.

Celebrating every step includes those steps, like optimism that work below deck. Yes, celebrate every win, every achievement, every goal, big and small. Most of all, celebrate the motivation that helps us achieve the next goal. The goal is always in sight, and our drive to accomplish it will seem to come effortlessly when our energies are aligned and positive.

Remember that discipline lives in a cyclical fashion. Discipline equals the power to be productive. Our job is to nurture our mindset so that we are empowered to obtain discipline, to master self-control and build successful habits.

Chapter 10: Confidence vs. Overconfidence

"The whole problem with the world is that fools and fanatics are always so certain of themselves, and wiser people so full of doubts."
– Bertrand Russell

So much of what we lack in discipline comes from what we lack in confidence. If we don't believe that we can be disciplined, what shot do we have of going at in earnest? Confidence is earned. When our *confidence bank account* is empty, we can't afford to be confident. When you think about it, this is a bad cycle to be caught in. Nothing in the tank to fuel our confidence and without confidence we can't fuel the tank (or make that deposit in the discipline bank).

How do we break a bad cycle? We need to do a couple of things simultaneously. One - we need to dig deep, find our courage and get ready to try again. Two - it's going to take a leap of faith. Faith that we will succeed this time despite what happened previously. There is a really important point buried in this last statement - "this time." This time is unique. That fact can fuel our desire, our courage and our faith to try again. This time has never happened before. We've never failed before at trying "this time." It's up to us whether or not to associate this time with the previous times. It's also up to us to disassociate it. Make the choice that this time is different.

Nobody has the right to tell us that we can't be confident this time.

Confidence Is a Skill

Confidence is a lot of things. It's a fear reducer, a courage provider and it's a skill. Confidence comes easy to some. Maybe it comes easy to people who were praised by their parents and others at critical times in their cerebral development. Maybe it comes easy to people who have been blessed with certain natural abilities, like being athletic or artistic. Maybe it comes easy to people who were lucky enough to be born with unusually physical attractive attributes. I can tell you from my experience that most people I've met who were born with special natural abilities, talents or beauty are no more confident than anyone else I've met.

I can also tell you that I've met tons of ordinary people who exude confidence because of their accomplishments. They've earned their confidence. This is what's meant when we say that confidence is a skill. Like other skills, you can hone your confidence, you can grow your confidence capabilities and you can make leaps in progress. Yes, you can start out with little confidence, become more confident, and then more so, and so on until you are extremely confident. This is a good thing. This means that you have the power, that you are in control of your own destiny.

Our experience teaches us that confidence is not one of those skills that you practice at in order to become better at it bit by bit. Confidence comes from our ability to put our mind to something and achieve it. Setting goals and achieving them will surely grow our feelings of confidence.

You Can't Fake Confidence

Trying to fake confidence is like cheating in golf, chess, dieting or any other activity. You might fool someone else, but you can't fool yourself. You know the real you - for better and for worse. You know your capabilities. You know what you deserve and what you've earned. That's how confidence works. There's really only one person who cares about your level of confidence, and one person who's terribly uncomfortable when it's lacking. Don't get me wrong. When I say you can't fake confidence, I'm speaking about the fact that you can't fake it to the degree that you believe you have it.

Trying to fake confidence is actually a common occurrence. You know people who do it reasonably well and people who do it poorly. Human beings have defense mechanisms that usually manifest subconsciously and affect how we move through the world. The most common confidence fakers are those who overcompensate and carry themselves as though they are supremely confident. Some are talented actors who are extremely effective in fooling the people around them. Think about the people you've met who are good at it. Maybe it's the CEO of the company you work at. Maybe it's your friend who can't help but brag about all the material possessions she's acquired. Maybe it's your neighbor who looks like Mr. Perfect, like he is the master of his universe, with never even a hair out of place.

If you don't ever get too close to a confidence faker, you may never learn that it's an act. However, if you experience enough time spent with this type of person, you detect that something is off. You'll notice inconsistencies, some cracks in the varnish. None of us are perfect, and those who work too hard to make you and everyone else think they are usually low on real confidence. Compare these people to the ones you know who don't puff out their chest and put on a big show. Time and again we see that the truly confident individual is understated. The confident individual has little need to try and impress; they don't need the adulation and have better things to do with their time than to try and get it.

Confidence and High Achievers

We know real confidence when we see it, at least in part because of measurable results. Think for a moment about someone you know who has made it the top of the ladder in their career. It could be someone you know personally or someone you don't, like a former athlete, artist or performer. Think about Olympic swimmer Michael Phelps. He'll be the first to tell you that when he was competing, if you put him in the water, his confidence was through the roof. He also would tell you that in other areas of his life, his confidence was sorely lacking. That's another part of confidence to consider, it's not absolute - that if you have confidence, you have it universally and if you lack it, you lack it everywhere. We know that not only does confidence vary from one aspect of life to another, but even in the areas where you're most confident - that confidence rises and falls from time to time.

When a professional athlete goes through a slump, his confidence takes a hit. The same is true for the corporate executive and everyone else. Something good happens and our confidence goes up, something bad happens and our confidence goes down. There's a saying about great pitchers in baseball, that they have a short memory. The point being that when they give up a home run - a result that means they've evidently failed - they move on with little remorse.

There are those whose confidence is so high, their mindset so strong, that the ups and downs supposedly don't affect their confidence level. I say supposedly because we'll never know. Even if they're not faking supreme confidence and they really have it, it's entirely possible that the ups and downs move the needle on their confidence level. In the case of a truly confident individual who believes that her confidence doesn't waiver, it's certainly possible that it does subconsciously - leaving her unaware of its movement.

High achievers are often noticed for the tangible talents and results, with little thought about what it takes to be successful at that level. In most cases, the term "mental toughness" applies. Mental toughness is likely a combination of many things, a mindset that supports confidence is certainly one of the more substantial qualities included.

Overconfidence

After giving so much consideration to the power and virility of confidence, you might think that there's no such thing as too much of it. Like everything else in life, there is a limit and there are balances - and yes you can have too much confidence. It's a human thing. When I was growing up, I lived in a household where both of my parents dieted frequently, striving forever, it seemed, to get to a better body weight. I remember the phrase, "You can't be too rich or too thin" uttered more than once. It was said in jest, but there's also a saying along the lines of, "Many a truth is said in jest." Well, we all know that while it's debatable whether anyone could be too rich, the same is not true for being too thin, which simply leads to death. Point being, too much of a good thing is not a good thing, and overconfidence is a detrimental mindset.

How do you know when you're crossing the line between being a healthy supremely confident individual to being overconfident? This seems to be a fair enough question. When does anything good become too much? When does participating in something healthy stop being healthy because we've taken it too far?

Let's have a look at physical exercise. For most of us, there's not enough time in the day or willpower to overdo exercise. When you think of it, this is a really interesting question. Let's consider the professional athlete. If you make your living from playing a sport and peak physical fitness is what you want, how do you know how not to overdo it. Sports trainers and sports medicine professionals likely have some scientific answers that speak to the law of diminishing returns and the point at which overuse injuries are sustained. In the case of the law of diminishing returns, it's simply a waste of time. The human body can only become so efficient before topping out. Muscles can only get so strong and the same is true of cardiovascular endurance. I think for our comparison to overconfidence, what's more relevant is the idea of sustaining overuse injuries.

Overconfidence Works Against You

The simple answer to the question about when it is that you cross the line from confidence to overconfidence has everything to do with results. Confidence as we know works wonders. It provides us with the motivation and comfort level to move forward when we otherwise might stall or quit. Overconfidence happens when we lose focus, get sloppy and think that the laws of nature might not apply to us, at least not *this* time. What we know about discipline is that it takes a special kind of mindset to use it. The mindset we need to be disciplined is fueled by the confidence that tells us we can do it. The overconfident mindset tells us that we take this particular workday off because something we want to do more is overriding our discipline in this instance. Now, don't get me wrong. If you've been working hard and need a personal day off of work, and it's not going to interfere with your performance and workplace goals, that's more of a planned event. It's even a planned event when spontaneous because in the back of your mind you've been thinking about it - you know it's there to be had - and it's accounted for. The spontaneous event that stems from overconfidence is one that ignores the laws of nature.

What's all this "laws of nature" stuff anyway? What it refers to is ignoring what's true, turning a blind eye, rationalizing, creating your own narrative. If the day off from work will impact your performance record, cause you to let someone down, jeopardize a timeline or the like - and you tell yourself that it will be fine, not a big deal - you may be trying to use your will to change what's true. If you believe that, your overconfidence is overriding your common sense.

Creating Your Own Narrative

One way to catch yourself or someone else acting with overconfidence is to acknowledge when the story being told about what's happening, what happened or what's about to happen is a story being told as a fact. Have you ever had a friend, relative or work colleague who is prone to this behavior? It's the type of thing that could make someone want to roll their eyes when hearing one of their stories. It could sound something like this from your Cousin Jerry:

> *"I'm starting a business that's going to change the world. You know how people love vegetarian food so much and there's just not enough of it in restaurants. I'm starting a line of recipes that professional chefs can use to make the most popular dishes using vegetables in place of animal protein. Restaurant companies will definitely pay top dollar for great recipes like this because the restaurant will now have more vegetarian options than ever, which means they'll be able to satisfy so many patrons who otherwise wouldn't order their food. Think about all the money they're leaving on the table. They will easily pay a lot for my recipes, and end up making more money as a result."*

You see what Jerry's doing right? Jerry is creating a narrative that works for him. He's making tons of assumptions about what's important and worthy to other people - and spouting these assumptions as though they are indisputable facts. Jerry's business idea may have merit. He may prove you wrong for rolling your eyes at him when his business takes hold and changes the restaurant industry forever. However, the laws of nature tell us that we are unable to predict the future. If Jerry wants to play it out and see what happens, that's one thing. If

Jerry actually believes his own narrative, he's suffering from overconfidence and may be really hurting himself.

Cousin Jerry's narrative may be extreme. It's to illustrate a point. What's important for us to consider is that sometimes we can be guilty of doing this on a smaller scale. Yet, regardless of the size of our narratives, if we can be mindful that we're telling a story that may contain leaps of faith or rationalizations, we can consider whether we are acting overconfidently.

Let's be clear that telling a story of how we hope things will play out, as a tool of inspiration - to visualize the future where we achieve certain goals - is different. The main difference is that one is built on aspiration and takes nothing for granted, while the other stems from overconfidence.

Overconfidence and Careless Mistakes

We all know that the danger of overconfidence is that it leads to mistakes. This is especially important when you're trying to master the power of discipline. If you've ever gambled before or tried to predict the outcome of your favorite sports team, you may know a thing or two about overconfidence. Las Vegas casinos love overconfidence. It's a big part of how gambling works. Whether you play a card game, choose a slot machine or gamble on a professional football game, here's how overconfidence works. You start with a theory, a strategy of might work. You get lucky and it works. That may give you some confidence, but do it long enough and have more success than you expected and suddenly you're overconfident. You think, if I just played cards for four hours and won $200,

I should double my bets and I'll have twice as much winnings four hours from now. The inexperienced gambler makes this mistake with great frequency, and so we have some very beautiful casinos in Las Vegas - they can afford to build them that way. You know the story about the next four hours of gambling. That's right, Mr. Overconfident hits a cold streak, and even after he starts losing, he reminds himself how smart his original strategy was and keeps going.

When it comes to discipline, remember all the things we need to line up in order to get good at it.
Focus is such an important component because it keeps us mindful of our goals, celebrating achievements large and small, and the like. Overconfidence makes us assume certain things that may not be true, which leads to careless mistakes that sabotage our ability to maintain discipline.

Regaining Your Confidence

As you can see, overconfidence is so completely different from confidence that it's almost hard to believe that they're so closely associated. In other words, it can be hard to believe that we traveled through the town of confidence to arrive at the strange land of overconfidence. How do we get back to that great place where we used to reside, when we were responsible, unassuming, and made fewer mistakes? It's an adjustment for sure, and the hardest part of making the transition is recognizing the state of overconfidence. Once we piece together that it's overconfidence that's to blame for our lack of discipline, we'll want to reign it in and get back to possessing the proper motivation that comes from real confidence. The trick is to catch ourselves acting with overconfidence. Look for the signs. If you find yourself rationalizing; saying things like, "One time won't break my momentum" or "Compared to her I'm doing okay" - you are rationalizing your behavior. If you find yourself telling a story of the future and using words as though it's factual, you're using a narrative. If you believe that you can get away with something that no one else gets away with, you're likely trying to force your way to an improbable solution and may be going against the laws of nature, which you know won't work out too well.

When you find yourself suffering the consequences of overconfidence, think about the virtues of humility and strive to take a more humble approach to things. You'll know when your confidence level is appropriate because of the results. Confidence is energizing in a way that's in balance with your abilities and the physical limitations of the world around you. Over-confidence and under-confidence have much in common, as both create suboptimal results. Whenever true confidence fails you, take action no matter how small. Get a victory. It could be cleaning your closet, learning a song on the piano, finishing a book, calling a good friend who pumps you up - anything that produces something positive that can jumpstart real confidence. You can build on it from there, just like you have so many times before.

Chapter 11: Accountability Wins

> "A winner is someone who recognizes his God-given talents, works his tail off to develop them into skills, and uses these skills to accomplish his goals."
>
> – Larry Bird

We all know people who not only exude confidence, but they actually crave the spotlight. Sure, there are famous actors for whom this analogy is literal, but in our everyday lives we see a similar dynamic play out. If you work in an office, you've seen people who love to have the opportunity to speak in front of the team when a meeting is called. You also know others in attendance who wish they could blend into the wall and hope that the meeting ends without them being called upon to speak. This dynamic is personality based most often and only sometimes correlates to floor time based upon merit.

Leaders are often comfortable speaking in front of a crowd, but being a good speaker or a suave presenter is not the same as being accountable. Great leaders are always accountable for their actions. Some are also accountable for the actions of their team. President Truman said "The buck stops here" and there's never been a better description of what accountability by a real leader looks like. Being accountable isn't just for leaders, generals, CEOs, stars, or any other high-profile individual. Accountability is more than an attractive trait, it's a healthy characteristic that every thinking person would be well-served to embrace.

Accountability is the anchor of discipline. It's you who wants to harness the power of discipline in order to accomplish your goals. Only can accomplish your goals and only you can achieve discipline for yourself. You can't buy it or have it gifted to you by an admirer. That's real accountability. When Oprah Winfrey decided to run a marathon, there were people who said, "She has so much money, she can afford trainers and professional chefs to make her healthy food, so she has an advantage." Anyone who knows anything about what it takes to run 26.2 miles knows that there's no advantage which can be bought by privilege that will help someone accomplish that feat. Oprah shrugged off the naysayers and basically explained that if she could have paid someone to do her training for her and run the race, that would have been great, but that not how you achieve a goal like that. Only she could accomplish it.

At the time that Oprah ran that marathon, she was already one of the wealthiest entertainers on the planet. She came from a humble upbringing and accomplished mind-blowing achievements. What did she have to prove to herself that was worth that effort? The answer is between Oprah and herself. The bottom line is that it was a physical challenge she wanted to take on, to prove something to herself, and it was only to her that she was accountable for getting it done. Nobody else would have faulted her for not doing it. It was a promise she made to herself, and there's no better motivating factor for embracing discipline than that.

Why Not Be Accountable?

From your experience, think about the people in your life who embrace accountability and those who shy away from it. I'm willing to go out on a limb and guess that those who embrace it are confident in their abilities and those who shy away from it are insecure. At the end of the day, it boils down to confidence. If you believe you're going to be successful, you'll embrace accountability. If you're accountable you get the accolades that come with success and the potential blame that comes with failure. The second part of this last statement is why some people shy away; they're petrified of failure and blame.

Most people who shirk their responsibilities when it comes to being accountable for how things turn out, are totally okay with missing out on the opportunity to claim ownership of any forthcoming success. Typically, they are willing to forego acknowledgement for a job well done, if it means they can skip out on any chance of being held responsible for a failed mission. I say "most people" and "typically" because there is a segment of people who are so unfair in their accountability structure, that they actually will claim no accountability – unless, or until, there is success and then they make believe that they were part of the risk/reward team all along. We look sideways at those people.

Leaders Who Avoid Accountability

Ideally, it should be rather unlikely that someone who avoids accountability could be in a position of leadership. Being a leader should inherently include the highest level of accountability, but there are leaders who "pass the buck." Leaders who deny accountability are generally poor leaders who are only in a position of power due to something other than merit. This could be true of a business owner who is the boss, but structures her company so that everyone else is responsible for outcomes. This way, when something doesn't go well, the boss can blame someone else and never has to take responsibility. This type of boss will typically take credit when things go right, of course.

Experience teaches us that leaders who avoid accountability aren't leaders at all. No one follows, or is inspired, by someone who won't be accountable. The truth is that leaders don't have an option when it comes to responsibility. The boss who hires other people and believes that they'll own the blame when things fail is wrong. By hiring these people and giving them responsibility, the boss has made a decision that should be based on her belief that they will succeed. It's her gamble and if they succeed, she's due the credit. If they fail, she shares in the blame, whether she accepts this truth or not.

Choosing to avoid accountability is like choosing to ignore gravity. If you drive a car off the edge of a cliff because you didn't see the end of the road ahead, there's no escaping accountability, or gravity for that matter. Life works this way in much less dramatic fashion every day. One thing that's absolute, if you intend to be a leader, then you more than anyone else, should grab the reins of accountability.

Accountability and Measurement

Whether you consider yourself to be a leader, a team player or a lone wolf, if you're breathing and your mind works, you are accountable. You may decide that there are situations where you choose not to participate because someone is seeking to make you accountable for success or failure for a situation where you don't have enough control over the process. This scenario describes one of those times where choosing to not be accountable makes sense because it's misplaced accountability right from the start.

There are times when a successful professional football coach is offered large sums of money to turn around a losing franchise, and the coach stipulates that he'll only take the job if he's also given the general manager position. The general manager of a football team is the one who decides which players to sign, who to cut, who to trade and who to acquire in trade from other teams. When the Super Bowl winning coach Bill Parcells was offered a job with the Dallas Cowboys years ago, he said he'd only take the position if they made him general manager too, claiming "If I'm going to be the chef, I want to buy the groceries." Coach Parcells knows all about accountability and he also knows that if he's going to commit to being supremely accountable he also needs to have supreme decision-making authority.

Coach Bill Parcells is known for another quote about accountability that speaks to accountability. It's related to the fact that sometimes coaches, players and fans will describe their team's accomplishments in vague terms. They may talk about how the team is getting better or "coming together as a unit." Sometimes they'll go as far as to say that they lost some close games that could have gone the other way or even go as far as to say, "we are a better team than our record states," as if they can frame how to interpret a record of twins and seven losses. Coach Parcells famously said, "You are what your record says you are" – putting to bed discussions about the nuances of wins and losses.

Sometimes we need to black and white lines of delineation to take away the ability to rationalize results, or worse yet, to "spin" them. Public relations professionals make a living off of blurring the lines, putting issues into the gray area whether they belong there or not, and then telling us the narrative they want us to believe. We know plenty about the value of other people's narratives, especially when focused on issues that can't be factually proven just yet.

When you need objective indicators to tell you how you're doing, how far along you've come thus far as you're traveling toward reaching a goal, create metrics if they don't already exist. If you're trying to lose weight, it's easy. You get on the scale at one point in time, then again after implementing your strategy, and you've either failed or succeeded depending on what the scale indicates. If you're trying to become a better songwriter, that's hard to measure if you're not doing it professionally. You likely need to assemble your own audience. It could be a small number of friends or family, provided you trust that they have the ability and willingness to be totally honest with you. That would give you a helpful measuring stick.

There's no right or wrong when it comes to creating measurement tools, provided that your intentions are pure, and you are able to be honest with yourself about their value. Sometimes we don't have the luxury of true black and white measurement, but can always create our own, put a steak in the ground, something that gives us a method for comparison so that we can assess our progress and be accountable. Upon measurement, we are accountable if we declare progress, lack of progress, or loss of progress - and we're willing to accept responsibility to make any changes needed to improve our process, continue on the path or create a new one, and measure again after the next period of time we decide upon.

Accountability and Commitment

Accountability is a trait that provides a wealth of value for those who embrace it. When we choose to be accountable, we can commit to a goal and manage our actions in a way that helps us honor that commitment. Without accountability any commitment made doesn't have a leg to stand on, it's a false commitment. Being accountable is a commitment we make - whether to ourselves or others. Confident people seek accountability. They know that by committing to something, they can hold their own feet to the fire. It can be a motivational tool. For the confident individual fear of failure is a great motivator. Unlike their counterparts who may freeze or fold under the pressure of accountability, the confident person is motivated to work that much harder.

Accountability is putting a steak in the ground. Commit to something and make yourself accountable for its success or failure. Put yourself on the line. Let's examine this last statement, what are you "putting on the line." What is it about accountability that sends some people running for the hills? What is rolled up in the perception of failure that scares the daylights out of some certain people. It's really about a sense of pride, reputation and self-esteem. When we boil it down to what's on the line, we can better understand why some people are willing to take certain risks that others aren't.

To the insecure person, the idea of being in the spotlight and failing is almost too much to bear. Insecure people care a lot, very likely too much, about what others think about themselves. For some insecure people, their very definition of themselves is built upon what they perceive others think about them. Understanding the mindset of someone who stands on such shaky ground, you can see why failure is terrifying. Wounded pride, reputational harm and diminished self-esteem can be a devastating blow to an insecure individual. They'd much prefer to sit out any opportunity for success if it allows them the opportunity to eliminate the risk of failure. The insecure person will avoid accountability at every turn. What's unfortunate for them is that the laws of nature include certain risks that come with living - and accountability is among them.

For the person secure enough to risk failure, accountability is a gift. It's a call to challenge. It's an opportunity for motivation. An opportunity to put fear of failure in its proper perspective - as an unavoidable part of living - and an opportunity to be driven by the desire for success. Undoubtedly, the opportunity of accountability is the opportunity to fully commit.

Chapter 12: Muscle Memory

"The good life is a process, not a state of being. It is a direction not a destination."

— Carl Rogers

When you seek discipline, what you seek is a way to embody a characteristic that gives you the power to commit, to follow through and achieve your goals. When we talked about intention in an earlier chapter, when we examined the habits of high achievers, we looked at the theory of "trust the process" because that's all you can control. When we consider muscle memory, it's an accomplished state that we arrive at because of the process we've employed to get there. The knowledge we obtain from studying; our ability to dribble a basketball; the dexterity we possess to create a chord and strum a guitar – these are the results of actions we've taken repeatedly in order to obtain.

What you accomplish today affects what you're able to accomplish tomorrow. Think about yourself critically for a moment and assess your ability to create a working process. Forget for the moment whether or not you're pleased with your track record of following through, just focus on whether or not you are process-oriented. If you're not, no worries, if you decide to become more process oriented there are plenty of resources for finding good ones, unless or until you are ready to create your own. The important part of having a process is having one that you can live with, one that you can commit to and envision yourself taking action within its framework.

Think about how important this is — to have a structured process that helps you establish good habits. Muscle memory is a goal. It means that we've established these good habits, we are comfortable with a workable process and we are in rhythm to the point that our helpful actions can be done almost automatically. I say "almost" automatically because we're human, our good habits are done mindfully and our accomplished muscle memory will diminish if we break the cycle of working the process.

The Destination Is the Journey

Think about what it takes to become a medical doctor. First you need good grades in high school to make it into a good college. In college you need good grades to get accepted to medical school. Once you complete medical school, you then have the privilege of getting more training in the form of a multi-year residency program and one or more internships where you specialize in your medical discipline. After all this training, where do you land? In a professional medical practice. It's called a practice because that's what it is. You don't sit back after all the accomplishment it took to become a medical doctor, you then work your practice, using the knowledge you've acquired within a structured process. You, the medical doctor, have landed squarely in your process; your destination and your journey are one in the same.

Discipline is an important part of working a successful process. If you don't have the discipline to follow through, the process falls apart. The process you choose should also be one that supports a disciplined and determined approach. The qualities, characteristics, motivators, and rewards we've discussed are all necessary components in a process that can thrive. When you create a new goal and a plan to achieve it, that plan should include details about your process. If your motivators answer the *why* questions, your process answers the *how* questions.

Think about a goal you're working to achieve. What are the good habits you're working to establish in order to reach your goal? What milestones and rewards have you set for yourself to acknowledge along the way? What support mechanisms do you have in place that takes the guesswork out of taking the next step?

If your goal is to lose 15 pounds, your process holds tremendous power for setting you up for success. The good habits you're going to establish may include some new rules around mealtimes. You may decide that there will be no snacking after dinner; or that you'll fill a plate with appropriate servings and not go back for seconds: or that dessert will be limited to 120 calories or less. To support these good habits, you'll need to buy the appropriate foods so that you can prepare meals that you enjoy, but also fall within the framework you've established. You may need to stay out of the kitchen once dinner is over, so that you're not tempted to snack. You may choose to reward yourself with the gift of new running shoes once you've lost five pounds, a celebration meal with larger dessert once you hit the 10-pound mark, and a great-looking new outfit once you've hit your goal of being 15 pounds lighter.

It's easy to see how a good process supports goal achievement. Each process we create teaches us about our ability to create a good one. Look at your process as you work it and make changes to improve whenever you identify opportunities for improvement. It's important to realize that some people are simply more process oriented than others. For some, creating and working a process is second nature – and they couldn't even imagine any other way to go about it. For others, the idea of working a process seems rigid and conflicts with how they perceive their creative nature. If you fall into the latter, use this opportunity to learn, grow and step outside of your comfort zone. This is also an opportunity to be creative, to build a more creative process than whatever you're envisioning that leads you to believe that this is a rigid and constrictive structure. Build a custom process unlike any other you would imagine - one that suits your personality and honors your lifestyle.

All that matters about your process is that it works for you. When you set out to achieve a goal, if it's set high enough, you don't know if you'll achieve it, regardless of your confidence level. What you do know is that you're embarking on a journey. We say that the destination is the journey because it's all we can control, all we can count on being available to us. When we set up a great process, it's easy to work it, and it's exhilarating. It feels good to be focused and determined. That's the reward that your process offers. When your process works, and you achieve "set it and forget" status, you move along the journey and somewhere along the way, you realize that you've developed muscle memory. Muscle memory tells us we've accomplished something very special.

Chapter 13: Momentum Theory

"It's fine to celebrate success but it is more important to heed the lessons of failure."

– Bill Gates

When everything aligns in support of your goals, it's a great feeling. You are motivated, working your process, achieving milestones, feeling productive and confident. You have momentum. Now, you have one question to ask yourself, "Is this sustainable?" If your answer is no, you can use the energy that emanates from that concern to make adjustments. When you adjust, you create something new. It's hard to imagine anything in this life of ours that is fully sustainable without adjustment.

Our ability to adjust to change is what helps us maintain a winning process. In many ways life truly is a game of chess. The board changes. Moves are made by a force other than you. If your strategy to win is inflexible, you're setting yourself up for loss because your strategy, which made all the sense in the world two moves ago, is now terribly flawed because of what transpired between then and now.

With the understanding that change is inevitable, we can be mindful of the fact that when something is moving along wonderfully, when our strategy and processes are producing the desired effect, in order to sustain it, we will have to make changes along the way. Too often, when things are working, we think our job is done here, just keep doing the same thing and we'll get the same results. This thought process appears to have merit because it seems to speak to the positive result of creating a working process. Do consider that nothing is sustainable without upkeep - and in the case of our winning process, upkeep includes adding motivators, changing up the rewards and setting new milestones.

A Body in Motion

This all revolves around Sir Isaac Newton's first law of motion. This law states, "A body at rest tends to stay at rest, and a body in motion tends to stay in motion, unless acted on by a net external force." When things are going well, and you're on a roll, think about this law and how the most difficult part of any initiative is getting started. Once you've managed to start, to continue, to work the process, defend this achievement by doing what it takes to keep it going. Keeping it going is easier than starting again because like Newton's law says "A body in motion tends to stay in motion."

To maintain a working process we need to call upon the power of discipline to do a number of things. First, we need to audit our process when it's working with the same focus we give it when it's broken. Secondly, we need to find room for improvement. The old saying, "If it ain't broke don't fix it," may work well for kitchen appliances, but when it comes to performance, the saying may be more helpful if altered to suggest, "If it ain't being fixed it, it'll soon be broken." See, we can keep the word "ain't" because it's so infrequent that this slang sounds "okay." Third, in addition to auditing and finding room for improvement, is to innovate. The best thing we can do to maintain a working process is to change it. Understandably, this sounds counterintuitive, but it's directly correlated with the fact that momentum will not sustain itself without intervention.

Momentum for the Next Step

When we speak about the value of using goal achievement to produce energy for taking the next step, we're talking about keeping the momentum going. We know that energy can be neither created nor destroyed, only transferred. So, when we put one achievement to bed, we have a couple energy-related opportunities at our disposal. The first is the fact that we can take the habitual energy we would have expended on achieving that goal and use for the next one. The other energy opportunity has to do with momentum. The positive energy we take away from achieving a goal is undeniable. It fuels our level of confidence, as "success breeds success." Directing this positive energy toward the start of the process for achieving the next goal is a way of sustaining the forward motion you've already established.

Momentum is about motivation. Once we become motivated, how do we maintain it? If your goal is to save money so that you can take a great vacation - like scuba diving off an exotic island, skiing in ritzy Aspen, or renting an RV and driving to the Grand Canyon - you've got plenty of motivation when you begin. You're likely willing to make sacrifices, liking shopping less or working more, because you have your eyes on the prize. If you create a plan that details the many ways you'll grow your savings account, you can put your head down, stay focused and make it happen. If it's a six-month plan, you may find the hard part to stay motivated happens around week three or four. You're making sacrifices and growing your savings, but there's still a long way to go and you start to feel bad for yourself because you're going without some things you really enjoy here and now. Can you pinpoint the moment you lost momentum? It's more likely than not a singular event that changed your mind. Something occurred that made you say to yourself for the first time since you decided on this goal that maybe it's not worth it?

It's at the first moment of doubt that your momentum is at peril. What sounds like a simple solution to regain your motivation is to try and recall what got you supremely motivated to set this goal in the first place, but that's easier said than done. The original motivation has waned, replaced by concerns about the sacrifice. The best way to stay the course and maintain momentum is look beyond the motivators that first come to mind and climb to the strongest motivation you have. Forget for a moment that the vacation will be incredibly fun, relaxing, exhilarating; what's at stake is the promise made to yourself.

You may be thinking, "I've broken promises to myself plenty of times, it's not beyond me to do it again." Fair enough. Though here's your chance to make a commitment that promises to yourself will not be broken. If you're okay with breaking a promise to yourself, then your promise is worthless. If your promise is worthless, then your sense of accountability, of being able to commit and of having the discipline to follow through are all shot. So, you see, your promise to yourself needs to be kept. If such serious commitment worries you, you can be more cautious about what promises you make and what goals you set. In doing so, you create a cycle of success - and the most important success you can find is in being true to yourself, and holding yourself accountable. In doing so, you become a master of discipline.

Chapter 14: A Slippery Slope

> "Even as you make progress, you need the discipline to keep from backtracking and sabotaging the success as it's happening."
>
> – Nipsey Hussle

Why is it that discipline, along with the commitment and motivations that foster it, are so difficult to maintain: We can point to a myriad of reasons, lack of focus, competing priorities, and general fatigue, are all perfectly good explanations. Yet, there's something more primal that simplifies the loss of discipline at any given time. It's negative thinking. It manifests itself in many forms - self-doubt, concern, insecurity, pessimism - it all boils down to allowing negative thoughts and the emotions that accompany them to dictate our actions.

We've all been there. Things are going well, your plan is being executed, you're experiencing good results - and you're feeling confident. Then something unexpected happens that causes you to doubt your beliefs. It could be something as simple as making a mistake or as big as realizing that your plan is ill-conceived and perhaps you have potentially wasted a whole lot of time. You get that twang of fear that signals to you that you're out of your depth, you bit off more than you could chew, and failure is imminent. This is a moment that you are either prepared for and have an action plan to counter these feelings, or you're about to get derailed in a big way.

Self-doubt can be a really tough thought process to break once it takes hold. If you've experienced it before and seen it unwind your opportunities for progress then you know about the downward spiral it can create. Doubt turns into fear and fear can paralyze you. What tactics can you think of to stop this cycle from taking hold? Here's one that is certain to be helpful - reach out to a trusted friend. Share what's going on. Slow down and listen. Fear has its way of winding us up. If we can catch ourselves feeling fearful early on, we can mitigate the fight or flight response that fear elicits. By reaching out to a good friend, you take yourself out of the flight response. Flight typically drives us towards isolation. Isolation is truly dangerous because it leaves you alone with your thoughts, and when you're in a negative mindset your thoughts can lead you to make bad decisions. Hence, the idea of reaching out to a friend. Do your own intervention.

Turning It Around

A good friend is glad to hear from you when you're struggling. A good friend cares and knows you well. He knows what you're feeling. He knows your fears, your shortcomings and your strengths. He also knows how hard you've worked to get the important forward motion necessary for reaching your goal. Remember that when you seek out a friend's advice, you'll have plenty of opportunities to share and be heard. You also should prepare yourself to listen intently. This can be a difficult thing to do when you're feeling overwhelmed. Be mindful of this fact so that you can prepare yourself to put aside the heaviest of your feelings, just for a bit, so that you can take in some much-needed wisdom. That's one more thing, do call on a friend whose advice you trust - someone you do see as wise, especially with regard to expertise in the area you're coping with right now.

Taking advice from anyone is challenging. You have preconceived notions about your capabilities and your comfort zone. When you're feeling fearful, you have already left your comfort zone. For the moment, accept that some of your best thinking, creativity and moments of growth happen when you are in this place. Your comfort zone isn't gone for good. You'll be back in it soon enough, but first, you may need to adjust your thinking a bit.

Remember that when you are in a time of struggle, if you put your goal achievement strategy on hold, you are not just standing still, you're moving backwards. I don't say this to put more pressure on you, but because it's simply true. When we're not moving toward our goal, we're moving away because time doesn't stand still. It's like being in a canoe and paddling towards your destination. There's typically a current involved. The current more often than not is moving against you, or pushing to one side of the other. Mathematically, if the current can be pushing in any direction at any given time, then the fact that it's not helping you is simply how it is seventy-five percent of the time.

All the more reason we need to stick to the old adage, "when the going gets tough, the tough get going." In times of struggle, remind yourself that this is where you have a unique opportunity to show your grit, to dig deep and to use your discipline when you *really* don't want to. The good news is that it's not such a stretch in thinking. Your discipline is all about doing what you need to do over what you want to do. It's about honoring the commitment you made to yourself. It's highly unlikely that when you set out to achieve your goal, you made some sort of agreement that sounds like this "I promise I'm going to reach this goal unless things get tough. If self-doubt comes along, I will abandon my efforts." Of course, you didn't say that because when you committed to your goal, you were motivated, and motivation comes with a positive mindset. This negative thinking has blindsided you, but you have the goods to overcome it as long as you anticipated that it wouldn't be all clear sailing the whole time.

Getting Centered

When doubt and fear hit, you're operating out of the emotional side of your mind. That's okay, especially if you recognize it, and if you also recognize that you also possess a rational side of your mind too. There's a behavioral therapy that's popular among mental health professionals that uses the term "wise mind" to describe the balance between the emotional and rational sides of your mind. The concept is that to operate with a wise mind, you want to be centered. You want to have the emotional side of your mind functioning in balance to your rational mind. This construct can be helpful if you tend to be more emotional or more rational than you care to be.

You may wonder, how can you be too rational? Well, if you know anyone who always operates in a cool and calculating manner, but is also a bit emotionally detached, you may say that this individual is operating too much from her rational mind and not enough from her emotional mind. Conversely the person whose actions are consistently driven by the emotional side of his mind would be well served to consider how to use more of his rational mind. The point of this is that when you are feeling emotionally overwhelmed with thoughts of self-doubt and fear, you may use this construct to see the imbalance and determine what you could do that would be more rationally driven so that you can be operating from the center of your wise mind.

Let's look at a simple scenario where you may be able to imagine yourself encountering an issue that has potential to create a negative mindset capable of throwing you off course. Imagine that your goal is to refrain from drinking alcohol for 30 days. One benefit associated with achieving this goal is getting an opportunity to see how it feels, especially if you're used to drinking a bit every week. Another benefit is fewer calories, enabling you to have a more nutritious diet, and the ability to reduce overall calories if weight loss is also an attractive outcome. Now, imagine that you're two weeks into the process and feeling good. The first week was tough, especially that first weekend, but you had the discipline and focus needed to establish a streak. Week two was not only easier, but you actually feel great. You may have lost a couple pounds and your mind feels sharper than usual. Then you slip up. An old friend drops over to tell you the good news about landing her dream job. She brings a bottle of wine from her favorite vineyard and asks you to join her in a toast. In a moment of weakness, you acquiesce. You end up having a couple glasses of wine.

Here's how you may feel when you wake up the next day, after having a couple glasses of wine. You may feel like you've failed. You've lost momentum that you worked hard to gain towards achieving your goal. You had a lapse in focus on the importance you placed on achieving this goal when you first set it. You're feeling a little foggy, because it's the first couple glasses of wine you had in a while, and to be honest, you're feeling sad. This is a critical moment. For most of us, our instinct is to feel bad, to feel like a failure, and worst of all to correlate it with other times we didn't have the strength and/or focus to complete a goal we set for ourselves. So, if you're in this category, you're in good company. I'd venture to say most people would feel this way. Here's the powerful truth about this moment. You have a choice available to you that is harder to accept, but will likely serve you best. Forgive yourself.

Forgive and Remember

You know what happens when you have a tiff with a friend and then you both decide that whatever caused the disagreement is not all that important. Though you know that it was actually his fault, so you say, "forgive and forget." If it really was a small issue, and there's no recurrence of the same or a similar event, you really may forget. That's not the case with your slip up that broke your streak and ended your attempt at achieving your 30-day abstinence from alcohol goal. You can't fool yourself into believing it's no big deal, because to you, it is. It's just one more time that you broke a promise to yourself, and now you don't know if you can trust yourself again. You can "forgive and remember.

You can trust yourself again if you own it, forgive yourself and get right back on the horse that threw you. Not easy, but very doable, with the right mindset. Let's remember that you have every "right" to adopt a defeatist mindset. Here's the thing, if you're in it for the win, go get a victory. The game is not over when you give up a home run in the fifth inning. Here's how you win. How even your toughest critic, you, will be impressed. You pledge to yourself that you will refocus your attention and go after this goal with more fervor than before. You make today day one of 30. You complete the 30 days of abstinence and not only will you have succeeded, but you succeed by a bigger margin. At the end of the next 30-day period you can look back and see that you've only had one day with alcohol over a span of 44 days, which should prove to be a bigger achievement for you. In addition to the obvious benefits that come from your success, you'll also have earned the elevated level of self-esteem and self-trust that come with achieving a goal that was once in doubt.

Forgive and remember what it felt like when you could have easily slipped into a cycle of self-doubt, poor motivation and lesser achievement. Most of us have battled such a cycle and still bear scars from the worst instances. At times when you feel low, it's more important than ever to embrace a plan that can help you work your way out. When you feel like you're getting down on yourself, see if you can turn that energy just enough to motivate yourself, even if it means calling yourself out. At the same time, practice self-compassion. You are trying, even when you fail. You are a motivated individual, even when you're fearful. In this world of ours you owe it to yourself to be your support system. You also owe it to yourself to lean on friends when you need to, knowing that you are there for them when they need you.

Dig in Early

When you've got momentum and you're feeling good, the best thing you can do to keep it going is to remain vigilant. That means being on the lookout for the let-down. Ask any behavioural health professional working the realm of addiction treatment and they'll tell you that lessons about staying vigilant are as important as any other wisdom they impart. They know all too well how quickly the gains a client works hard to achieve can quickly be reversed by a lapse of focus, determination and discipline. One of the best terms I've heard about catching a problem before it manifests is this: "The relapse happens before the relapse." What it means is that before someone deviates from their hard-earned sobriety, they've psychologically started to do so. In other words, if they could just stay mentally focused and determined, the seed of deviation would not have the ability to grow.

When you're goal oriented and seeking the discipline you need to maintain hard earned gains, be vigilant about holding on to what you've gained. Pay attention to your confidence level, and if it's falling, realize that it leaves you vulnerable. Without the right level of confidence, the seeds of self-doubt have room to grow. We all know what happens when self-doubt takes hold. We say that the backslide is a slippery slope for a reason. If you can rationalize one bit of relaxed discipline, you can rationalize another. Before you know it, you've lost valuable momentum.

Staying vigilant is all about staying focused. Think about those times in life when you've been hyper focused. What was it that led to that state of being? What did it feel like, and what did you accomplish when you were in that state? Just as we carry with us the baggage from failures we've experienced, so too can we be sure to carry forward the memory of every achievement that made us who we are today. Don't ever give more credence to your past failures than you give to your past achievements. Remember that what we focus on impacts how we think. How we think affects how we feel about ourselves - whether we feel confident or insecure - accomplished or doomed for failure. Being positive and optimistic is a choice, just like negativity and pessimism. The fact that you have this choice – that your mindset is not a game of chance or in the hands of outside factors – is a very good thing. This fact is one that we should never take for granted and always do our very best not to forget.

Chapter 15: The Discipline to Try Again

> "It is not the strongest of the species that survives, nor the most intelligent that survives, but the one most responsive to change."
>
> – Charles Darwin

Discipline is all about effort. It's also a skill that takes continuing practice for us to master to the best of our ability. Like everything else in life, it requires a continued effort to not only gain forward progress, but to maintain what's been achieved so far. Arguably, the only part of an endeavor more challenging than taking the first step is the act of taking the next step once you've suffered a setback.

Mindfulness experts know all too well about the discipline of trying again. A foundational principle of meditation practice is the act of beginning again. If you meditate or have ever tried meditation, you likely understand how important this is to the practice. What the newcomer to meditation often feels when he finds his once focused mind has begun to wander is something along the lines of *"I'm not doing this right."* If someone is available to guide him, they'll be quick to explain that he is indeed doing it right. Practice is inclusive of successful focus giving way to a wandering mind. The goal is to become better at sustaining longer periods of focus where the mind does not wander as often, but even the best trained meditators experience this occurrence. The advice they give to the person who is new at meditation is the same advice they take themselves "When you notice your mind wandering, simply, gently, begin again."

Well, that sure sounds simple. Almost too simple, right? But, what other explanation could you possibly give? I guess there is another option; one that people take all the time, give up. Walk away and say to yourself, "I can't do this. I'm not good at this kind of thing. This always happens."

The negative and defeatist thoughts are almost always driven by our fear of failure - and our desire to simply stop trying rather than face the very good possibility of failing again. Here's the thing that you and I both know to be true – the only way to get anything done is to be willing to work at it, and working at it includes failing, even if briefly, and starting again.

Trying Again Is Core Work

If you're familiar with a method of physical fitness training called Pilates, you know all about working your core. The Pilates method was developed by Joseph Pilates and it focuses on exercises that strengthen the core muscles of the body, with the understanding that whatever strength and flexibility an individual is seeking, it must begin with a powerful core. The torso contains many of the body's core muscles, and with a strong torso, it's easier to maintain good posture and have optimal technique for any other exercise.

With the Pilates analogy in place, let's think about how building strong "try again" muscles hold the key to a powerful approach to discipline. Keep in mind that trying again is not only important when we fail, it's important when we are successful too. As we covered in our discussion of momentum theory, the finishing of one goal provides energy, motivation, and confidence to begin the next. Of course, no matter how confident or motivated, beginning the next goal is another form of trying again. Perhaps more germane to our thinking of trying again as related to success is the fact that we humans are imperfect. So, even when we are in good rhythm, building and commencing with good habits, and finding success – there is typically the need to do it again, trying again to do it even better, striving for perfection.

The important distinction being made is that "trying again" may be ingrained in our brains as an ancillary part of a process, but in the discipline game, it's an essential player. If discipline were a large employer reacting to a dangerous winter storm by announcing, *"only essential workers need report to work,"* try again would need to report. Okay, so you get it, trying again is important.
When you think of it in these terms, it's obvious, nothing substantial gets done with the discipline required to try again.

Sometimes we need an example to help us make this connection beyond words on a page. When you hear the backstory of many famous people, they'll tell you how difficult it was trying to become a success, and that they credit someone or something for motivating themselves to try again. J.K. Rowling, who's Harry Potter books have sold more than 50 million copies, was a single mother living on government assistance during the time she wrote the first book in the series. When she completed it, she was turned down by the twelve largest publishers before she tried again and got a smaller publishing house to say, "yes."

Thomas Edison, the well known inventor of the lightbulb is said to have failed 10,000 times in his attempt to create one that performed well enough to be produced and sold. Asked about how he was able to sustain his try again attitude while failing so many times, he replied, "I have not failed 10,000 times or even once. I have succeeded in proving those 10,000 ways will not work." How's that for a positive frame of mind? It's hard to think of a more inspirational way of viewing a failed attempt. It's not a failed attempt at all if it's a learning opportunity - and when you think of it - isn't that exactly what every attempt hands you?

The Try Again Mindset

Discipline is easy when we embrace a mindset that has us prepared. Prepared to bring positivity and confidence to the table and prepared to work harder when those qualities temporarily escape us. Edison could have quit after the first failed attempt, or the second, or the 9,999th. No one could have blamed him. Many would have said "that poor man finally stopped wasting his time with that electric lightbulb thing." They may have even rationalized that candlelight is more than fine (especially if you have a family member in the candle making business). For Thomas Edison, discipline didn't even feel like discipline - but it was.

People like to say "Do what you love for a living and you'll never have to work a day in your life." I like the sentiment, and believe it says a lot about the power of positive mindset, but there's no silver bullet that makes everything easy. Think about what you consider a dream job. Maybe it's being a professional musician and touring the world, getting on stage, and entertaining. I think we all know that no matter how talented, it takes practice to perform at a high level – and there are plenty of days where finding the motivation for a strong practice is work. Maybe you think a dream job is being a talk show host and interviewing interesting people; being a famous chef and developing award-winning recipes; or maybe it's being a scientist and chasing the cure for cancer? Can you see how any of these pursuits may make it easier to find and sustain motivation, but that none could be maintained without effort and discipline?

There's nothing wrong with having a job that feels like a big chore, or an uphill climb on any given day. There's nothing wrong with having a hobby that challenges you, or makes you feel defeated because you can't see real progress some days. That's when you have the opportunity to dig in and prove something to yourself. *If it was easy, everyone would do it.* If that was the situation, then it wouldn't be very rewarding. We need challenges in our life. We need the right mindset to be ready to meet the challenge – win, lose or draw. Without a real challenge, one that includes a formidable foe that we know as failure, we miss out on an opportunity to grow; to win. There's no such thing as win that comes to us without the chance of a loss. The mindset that says, "I'm going to get this done, just try and stop me," is the mindset of try again. We will come up short. If the challenge is big enough, we'll come up short time and time again. Try again is all we have. It's also all we need.

Chapter 16: Being Vulnerable

"Imperfections are not inadequacies; they are reminders that we're all in this together."

– Brené Brown

Vulnerability is a prerequisite for trying to accomplish something that may leave you feeling worse off emotionally for having tried and failed. Vulnerability is stepping outside your comfort zone into that place where failure is possible. If your fear of failure is sizable then so too is your fear of being vulnerable. Understanding this is important because it lives at the base of quitting, not trying, and rationalizing that there's nothing wrong with going that route. If you fear being vulnerable and don't confront that fear then you will have a hard time mastering discipline, building and sustaining better habits, and achieving your goals.

Who wants to be vulnerable? You might think that the logical answer is "nobody." That's not the case. Researcher Brené Brown has done a spectacular job of bringing understanding about vulnerability to light over the past decade or so, and one of the things she discovered is that there are people who embrace vulnerability because they recognize the benefits of doing so. Most importantly, being vulnerable is a part of life. When we work to avoid being vulnerable, we become a part of the segment of people who choose to sit this one out rather than take a chance. We know that discipline requires commitment, and commitment requires some level of risk, so working our way through this chain of logic; if we refuse to be vulnerable, we're going to be unsuccessful in being disciplined about anything important enough that it helps us reach a properly set goal.

Life Rewards Vulnerability

Think for a moment about a dramatic film you've seen that blew you away. If you've ever been in awe of the commitment an actor made to portray a character in a way that made it incredibly believable, that effort likely included the embracing of a vulnerable state of being. Actor Woody Harrelson explained in an interview that after playing a particularly dark character in one of his films, that it took him more than half a year to bounce back from the mental state he had put himself into. This is an extreme case, but it's a good example that there are real life risks involved with vulnerability.

In your life, you may never do anything to make yourself as psychologically vulnerable as a character actor playing a criminal, but you have felt the heart-pounding effects of being vulnerable and you've experienced the joy that comes from having been courageous enough to proceed despite your fear. If you've ever asked someone you really cared about to go on a date, or if you said "I love you" to a love interest before being 100% sure of the response, you know vulnerability well. Even those times you put yourself out there, and got rejected, you felt a sense of pride by being strong enough to take a chance. As is the case with any sizable gamble, experiencing success will embolden you to do it again, and losing can shake your confidence considerably.

Insecure people will usually refuse to put themselves in a vulnerable position. They gladly forego a chance at winning in order to avoid a chance of losing. They convince themselves that by doing so they are neutral; they're game ends in a tie. But, we know better and they know better. Trying a losing puts you further ahead than the individual that sits it out, if for no other reason than the fact that losing teaches us something. Failure puts us a step closer to success more often than passing on effort.

Just to be clear, life rewards vulnerability because life rewards action. We all have thoughts about pursuits we'd like to try or accomplish that we believe we don't have time to begin putting a plan into action just yet. Sometimes, we are right to hold off on them because we are taking care of higher priorities first. Other times, we're simply putting them off because we like the dream of what could be better than finding out whether or not we have what it takes to achieve one of those goals. Obviously, we have to live with the consequences of not trying if we never make time to pursue these dreams of ours. Sometimes, when we see others pursuing their dreams, we are envious if we're not doing the same. There is a solution that allows us to feel good about putting certain goals on hold until we have the bandwidth to begin with the right framework, including the right frame of mind. That solution is intention.

As long as we acknowledge that we are taking care of our highest priorities first and keeping certain pursuits "in queue" then we're being mindful of our intentions. Not yet with intention is very different from not now because I'm scared. Vulnerability is such an important quality to embrace because it's a litmus test that tells us we're not living completely in our comfort zone and that we are taking appropriate risks. Ask yourself periodically whether you feel vulnerable – and if the answer is no – you know it's time to try something new and unproven. Remember that life rewards action. Golfers famously say, "100% of the puts that don't reach the cup don't go in." We can draw a lot of wisdom out of this saying. If you're trying to sink a put and you don't hit the ball hard enough to reach the hole, you've not given yourself a good enough chance to put it in. Now, that's not to say that aggression is always to be rewarded either. The golfer who hits each put hard because she doesn't want to come up short will also be the golfer who hits it so far past that hole that it takes two more strokes to finish up. So sometimes the ball not reaching the hole is not a bad thing, if you've put it close enough where your probability of success on the next put is very high. The point of this story is to always give your best effort – and take into account your risk-reward probabilities too. Just be mindful of the effort you give, and you can feel good about the outcome, whatever it is.

Vulnerability and Courage

Of course, it takes courage to allow yourself to be vulnerable. When you find yourself having a hard time mustering the courage it takes to be vulnerable, take a moment and figure out what's so frightening about putting yourself out there. There's so much to learn in these moments. If you're a perfectionist, this fear will slap you in the face in a way that the person less concerned with perfectionism will not have to endure. If you know yourself to be a perfectionist, you're going to see that in order to be vulnerable enough to participate through times of discomfort, that for you that means you're going to have to put "perfect" to bed and join the rest of us.

You already know that as humans we don't get to choose a perfect life. It just isn't going to work out that way. It's about control, right? Well, here's the good news, you get to control a lot. You can control your effort, your plan, your commitment, but none of it comes without being ready, willing and able to fail. This is where you get to control your decision to be courageous. As Brené would say, "to show up, to be seen." This is a challenge you are more ready for than you give yourself credit. Of course, you don't feel quite ready just yet, but you're smart enough to know that nothing will change that will make you ready to be uncomfortable, and vulnerable, tomorrow as opposed to today. At some point, despite the fact that we know the pool water is going to feel too cold at first, we jump in because we want to swim, or get cooled off, and we know it will get better. That's the leap of faith required for being vulnerable.

We all have different levels of perfectionism within us. It's a sense of pride. We all want to be successful. Certainly, none of us want to be branded a failure. Here's an important point; failing doesn't make you a failure. Thomas Edison failed, Michael Jordan failed, Bill Gate failed. Everyone fails. Nothing leads to failure with more consistency than not trying. Success belongs to those with the courage to try and to be vulnerable.

Another thing researcher's discovered about vulnerability is that it's required in order to connect with others. This makes a lot of sense when you consider that those who shy away from vulnerability tend to isolate because there's nothing that makes us feel more vulnerable than interacting with others, and feel like we're being judged. It's important to understand that you are not alone in feeling this way, and therefore you're not alone in needing to summon the strength to be vulnerable.

We all recognize the universal truth in this phrase: "There's strength in numbers." In the physical sense, this is obvious. If you're trying to overtake a government or any regime, you have a better chance of doing so if you have the majority of people on your side. This phrase is also true from a psychological perspective. If you're the only one finding the courage to be vulnerable, that feels much more frightening than if you consider that everyone else who is seeking to achieve great things requires courage as well. It's easier to do something when we can see examples all around us of others who are finding the courage to do it. That's how it is with vulnerability.

As human beings, our experiences around issues of vulnerability and insecurity may be surprisingly more universally shared than we could ever imagine. It can be hard to believe that the same insecurities you feel are truly experienced by others. After all, you are such a unique being. No one else could possibly share all of the specific psychological issues you have that are the result of your individual experiences. Yet, there are plenty of insecurities and vulnerabilities that unite us.

Take for example, Imposter Syndrome. This term was introduced by psychologists in the 1970s and it includes feelings that many share, at least at certain times in life. If you've ever felt in a position of authority that you didn't think you properly earned: or have been celebrated for an achievement that you thought you "lucked into" or had been given credit for an accomplishment for which you didn't feel worthy – you have suffered from Imposter Syndrome. For a great many people, hearing that this feeling is a shared phenomenon is comforting. It could naturally be assumed that this sensation, of feeling like an imposter, uniquely belongs to you, the individual. Understanding that your fears are not unique can be enlightening and even empowering enough to give you the courage to confront these uncomfortable, and misplaced, feelings.

Doing whatever it takes to get comfortable with vulnerability is the goal. In order to make a commitment about something meaningful in your life, something that you'd hate to fail at, you're going to need to embrace vulnerability. Being able to make this commitment sets the wheels in motion. When you can commit, you can try because you're able to withstand your fear of failure. Once you can commit, you're worthy of making a sizable promise to yourself and doing the work it takes to demonstrate determination. With this foundation in place, you are set to embrace discipline and enjoy the power that comes with doing what you say you're going to do.

Chapter 17: What Winning Looks Like

"Do the best you can until you know better. Then when you know better, do better."

— Maya Angelou

We've done a reasonable amount of exploration about how fear can stand in your way. Fear and insecurity can be terribly demotivating and take you swiftly off track, often by working through your subconscious mind, so the purpose of that focus is to get you ready. When you're prepared, you are a capable foe. Now, let's get on to the good stuff. Chasing the outcome you desire because you're heading toward the light. Your shining North Star, what you really want, will keep you moving in the right direction, especially if you can vividly envision what your success looks like, feels like, sounds like, smells like, and tastes like.

Some people have a more vivid visual imagination than others. If you know you want something, but you literally can't bring yourself to imagine how to experience it with your senses, that's okay. You can find a suitable replacement for your own imagination. This is where our role models come into play. If you can think of someone who has achieved a goal same or similar to the one you're pursuing, seeing them clearly can be a suitable placeholder for now. It's still best to use your senses and do some imagining. What do you think he feels to have achieved such a lofty goal? Imagine the sense of pride and satisfaction. Imagine the confidence.

Let's not fool ourselves about the feeling you experience when you achieve a great goal. Depending on your mindset, and what other goals you have in mind, you may not savor it for long. Oftentimes we get so caught up in bigger and better that we have a hard time stopping to smell the flowers. If you have this impulse, to quickly check off the box of an achievement and begin working on the next, do stop yourself, even if just a bit longer than usual, to savor it. If we're unable or unwilling to appreciate our achievements, it may work against our ability to sustain motivation for the next goal. If you ever find yourself in a mindset of "Nothing really matters anyways" it simply means you're experiencing burnout, and it's time to recharge your batterie and reestablish your drive.

The Winners Circle

Let's face it, winning is all about self-esteem. Whatever other benefits accompany the achievement of your goals, none compares to that feeling of achievement, of winning, of being a winner! Success not only breeds success, it also breeds confidence. It's not too far a stretch to equate your status as an achiever with the status of other achievers, regardless of magnitude of either accomplishment.

If you love watching entertainment award shows, such as The Grammy Awards, The Academy Awards ("The Oscars"), The Television Academy Awards ("The Emmys") or The Tony Awards, you may appreciate the camaraderie. Not that there's anything wrong with watching for the speeches and the fancy dresses, but there's a sense of community among those accomplished artists that's hard to miss. They've all experienced success at a very high level. They also achieved success at lower levels in order to make it to the highest echelons in their profession.

If you are disciplined, determined and a successful goal achiever, you share what they share – a sense of self-esteem and value that is beyond what any award can provide.

The winning feeling is a result that can't be manufactured, in other words it can't be faked. It's a feeling that is sweetest when it rewards a process that includes discipline and courage. Courage because winning is only impressive when it includes overcoming obstacles, the obstacle of creeping negative emotions tied to thoughts of failing, of coming up short, are almost always among those needing to be conquered for victory. Yes, winners get treated differently, and that can be a nice result too, but it's nothing compared to feelings of self-worth and confidence.

Winning Is Addictive

Once you've tasted the type of win that's associated with overcoming serious obstacles, that type of satisfaction is something you'll want to experience again. It's the best motivator to drive plan setting and partaking in the good habits needed to achieve the next goal. The winning addiction can be a very good thing, as long as you remember that the goal is actually the journey. The way you spend every day leading up to the pinnacle of goal achievement defines how you're living. Being hyper focused is great for a sprint, but if it excludes other ambitions and responsibilities that matter to your wellbeing, then it's best that you keep it in check.

Workaholics are chasing something. If you work hard for a two-week sprint, working nights and weekends to make an ambitious deadline, that's commendable. When you work nights and weekends month after month, year after year, you are obviously out of balance and not maintaining what's needed in other parts of life. As you pursue your dreams, be mindful of what you're sacrificing, be sure to have boundaries, and take an honest look at whether changes to your personality are for the better or worse.

When you're chasing honorable goals, more often than not the changes that occur in your life are changes for the better. It's a wonderful byproduct of value-driven goals. If you chase goals with little forethought about the habits required to achieve those goals, and how those habits will change you, then you're much like a sailboat without a rudder – and you would be right to be concerned about where you'll end up.

With mindful decision-making, you can embrace the best parts of winning addiction and steer clear of those that are detrimental.

Making Clutch Plays

When you're winning, your confidence is sky high. If you're a confident basketball player, you're the one looking to take the buzzer beating last shot when your team is down by a point. You realize that you'll be on the one responsible for the loss if you miss the shot. You also realize that you'll be responsible for the win if you hit it. What's great about the winning mindset is that you know you are capable. There's no reason to pass up that last shot if you're feeling confident. Someone must take it and you're as mentally prepared and well-trained as anyone else, maybe even better. Missing the shot will not make you a loser. It will prove you're brave and that you have leadership qualities. The winning mentality means that you'll be ready to take the last shot of the game once again, even if you miss it this time, and that next time, you're prepared to win or lose once again, without it changing the status of who you are.

This is what winning looks like. It's about being confident and focused on the process, not the result. You know that that result is sometimes beyond your control. Putting in the effort, being prepared, being resilient and focused, these are the things you can control and it's during the times when you prepare as if the game is on the line that you're carrying yourself like a winner.

The good habits you'll foster to reach your goals will likely have nothing to do with training for a sports event. Partaking in your good habits is your training to be ready for your big moments. Making the clutch play for you is digging deep when the pressure is on and your decision making is either driven by discipline or copping out. The cop out is giving in to your rationalization – "just this time, just one day off, just one piece of cake, just a weaker effort today." The clutch play is staying laser focused on your goal and saying no to the easy way out. Every time you feel the urge to give in, realize that this is a clutch moment. You either step up or give in. Your choice. You know what winning looks like, so it's a very hard choice to make. Usually, when you make the choice not to try and make the clutch play, it's because you lose focus and take the easy way out by habit. More often than not, it happens subconsciously and quickly – and only afterwards do you realize that you missed an opportunity to win today.

Remember that winners have an off day, a day where they make the wrong choice due to fatigue distraction or something else that makes them miss an opportunity. When you fail, you have another chance to be a winner. Treat yourself with compassion, let the failure roll off your back, try again and regain your winner's composure.

Winners Take Decisive Action

Every goal starts with decisive action. You think of something that you want, and you realize it's worth working for it. You're excited and highly motivated, and you make the grand statement:

- "I'm going to do this."
- "I'm going to get straight A's this year"
- "I'm going to lose 25 pounds"
- "I'm waking up early and exercising before work"
- "I'm learning to play guitar"
- "I'm going to save $5,000"

These declarative statements feel like decisive action, but we know better. The decisive action begins when you put together a plan for success. Decisive action happens when you show up like you said you would. Decisive action happens when you say no to distractions and yes to that which motivates you along the way.

Winning Is A Mindset

Let's be clear about how we think about the terms "winning" and "winner." These are constructs to be used for the sake of clarity and goal motivation. If you choose to use these concepts for help in creating better self-control and better habits, that's great. At the same time, it's healthiest to refrain from seeing the world in binary terms of "winners" and "losers." It can be dangerous to label yourself as either. Call yourself a winner and you're likely to become overconfident. Never call yourself a loser, even for reasons of motivational challenge (calling yourself out) because words have power, and you are too good to engage in defeatist name-calling.

Let winning and winners serve to inspire you only. Let these terms help you gain clarity when things get foggy and making good decisions becomes difficult. Do step outside of yourself and imagine how someone you admire would approach your situation. Use these terms for a sense of perspective, but always realize that you can fail and never be a failure, because you're always willing to try again.

At any point in your life, including your lowest, you can turn it around fast if you're willing to adopt the mindset of a winner. That mindset is simply one comprised of courage, confidence, commitment, determination, and discipline.

Chapter 18: Discipline Mastery

> "One thing I've learned is that I'm not the owner of my talent; I'm the manager of it."
>
> – Madonna

Discipline is either present or absent in the choices we make. Do you wake up today and do what you said you were going to do, or do you do something else? At the heart of discipline is our ability to follow through on that which we've committed to previously. How much do you care about the promises you make? Does it vary depending on who you promise? Is it determined on the size or magnitude of what's at stake?

As you can see, discipline requires that we ask ourselves some hard questions, and that we don't stop there, we answer them. Answer the questions above and think about whether or not your answers are aligned. Are they consistent with one another or do they conflict, does one undermine the sincerity of another? If they don't align, reconsider them and see if you can answer them so that they are consistent. Think about core strength and posture. If you're not aligned, you're not performing optimally. Giving extra thought and changing an answer or two may clue you in to an important piece of your discipline-maintaining puzzle.

When we think about discipline lightly, it seems like a simple enough choice to create a life where discipline is a central component. Easy-peasy, right? Well, then life gets in the way.

Before you know it, conflicts arise between what you've committed to in relation to new stimuli. It's almost unfair when you think about it. You commit to doing extra work this weekend, so that you can catch up on something important. Then you learn that your best friend from high school is in town and wants to get together, and it's been years since you've seen her. When you made your commitment, this new stimuli was absent from the picture, but now you seem to have to choose between honoring your commitment (flexing your discipline muscles) or doing what you really want to do, seeing your old friend. Of course, your mind jumps to "Well, maybe I can do both?" Maybe you can, depending on how much work you intend to do and what else you can move around in your schedule.

So powerful is discipline that it can help you have your cake and eat it too, so long as you're willing to sacrifice enough other things in return. In order to do the work you intended to do this weekend and spend time with your good friend, you'll need to wake up earlier than intended to get a good block of work done. This is during a time period you may have reserved for sleeping in, working out, or doing something else you had planned. Discipline is what allows you to hang out with your friend, but for a shorter period of time than you may wish, or to be sure that you skip on that glass of wine because you're going to do work when you get home later.

Is Discipline Mastery Possible?

Of course it is! There's evidence of it everywhere. To clear up any potential confusion, the title of this chapter, "Discipline Mastery," is accurate, but it's important to understand that mastery is a practice, it's not about absolute perfection. Eric Clapton is most certainly a guitar master, but he would easily admit that he can never master the instrument perfectly – there simply is no such thing. Even if you find Clapton's playing to be perfect (*it sounds that way to me*), take into consideration that he's mastered many chords and notes that can be played in infinite arrangements that produce wonderment. That doesn't mean he can perfectly play songs in a jazz, classical or flamenco style. Even playing the blues, Eric "slow hand" Clapton may confide that there are techniques he uses more perfectly than others.

With ideals of perfection out of the way, discipline mastery is available to anyone willing to put in the effort, and maintain focus. Discipline mastery is no real secret, it's about drive. If you can tap into that which drives you to commit and show up, discipline is within reach. If you don't know what could possibly drive you strongly enough to impact your discipline ability, then this is the place to start. Why is it that you're supremely motivated to do certain things and not others? Obviously, you're more motivated to do the things you enjoy doing, but might it also come down to the fact that those things come easy to you. To master discipline, up your focus on the things you know you should be doing that you're not. Most likely, what those things have in common is that they're not "in your wheelhouse," meaning that they don't come easy to you. Yet, you know that embracing those challenges are what discipline is all about. Discipline is often about doing what you don't feel like doing because it's your path to a goal that you want to achieve.

Discipline mastery hinges on our ability to be mindful of the larger goal we've set for ourselves, and to act with determination to achieve it. Discipline mastery means that we do today what we'd prefer to do tomorrow, when we know that tomorrow holds no magic power for us that today is devoid of. Eric Clapton didn't practice for hours on end because it was easy, he did it because he was driven. When you have drive, or a calling from within you to achieve something, it's a gift. Find that part of you. It's a gift because it offers you the energy to get started and to sustain a good effort just long enough for you to develop muscle memory for the discipline required for the long haul. That muscle memory enables you to require less and less motivation to sustain your efforts. It's like the fuel that runs your motor, and with enough fuel, your motivation need only throw a spark to ignite that fire. Simply align your determined spirit with a magnetic goal and you are rolling down the road to discipline mastery.

Discipline and Maturity

Discipline can help you have more of what you want, provided you're willing to live in balance with the laws of nature. In the example above, where there's seemingly a choice between doing the work we committed to previously or spending quality time reengaging with a friend, maturity helps us make a good choice. Maturity is a quality that we typically ascribe to those who have had more experiences than others. Frequently, maturity does come with age and experience. Yes, there are plenty of aged and experienced people who act immaturely and plenty of young people who are incredibly mature. What this tells us is that maturity is really a mindset. It's a willingness to forgo immediate gratification in order to adhere to a commitment, or principled way of being, that's been previously agreed to.

Maturity can take us a long way on our journey to being more disciplined in our efforts because we are more willing or more understanding of trade-offs. The mature individual understands that we don't get to have it all and that in the world of gambling, "the house always wins." The mature outlook on life's events reminds us that there will be another great opportunity for fun around the next corner. It reminds us that sacrifice does pay off and that we are not depriving ourselves when we make a decision to remain focused on a long-term goal rather than choosing a short-term gain. Maturity informs us that what we do today affects the position we are in tomorrow. A mature outlook keeps the benefits of discipline front and center when the part of our brain that prefers immediate gratification is doing its best to steal our attention.

As you work to master discipline and self-control, be grateful for the maturity you possess. Pay attention to your maturity; honor it and nurture it. It's hard to imagine mastering discipline without a substantial reserve of maturity nearby.

Discipline and Self-Control

Self-control embodies many things, not the least of which is the ability to have some control over our emotional state of being and our actions. We often think of discipline in terms of how it materializes in the physical world. Having the discipline to do chores, practice an instrument, or exercise when we would prefer to be doing something else, is a common way we think of discipline being applied. What about the discipline we have over our mind? Surely the discipline to think about things that we know to be healthy for our mental state – and turn our thoughts away from issues that fuel negative thinking is supremely helpful. Discipline and self-control walk hand in hand whether the outcomes we seek are manifested in the physical world or not.

Mastering discipline includes mastery of the mind. With all we've uncovered about the role that fear, insecurity, and vulnerability play in sapping our energy, it seems obvious that we cannot master discipline without the ability to exercise control over our thoughts in general. Let's remember that nothing we talk about in this regard is absolute. No human being gets the privilege of ultimate mind control. Our subconscious mind puts that idea to bed. What we can do is make inroads.

Applying discipline to our thinking is not the same as controlling our thoughts. In other words, as any mindfulness expert will attest, we do not have control over the thoughts that enter our mind, but we do have control over how we perceive those thoughts and where we put our attention. Mindfulness exercises, including different types of meditation, often suggest that we see our thoughts coming and going as if we are watching trains come in and out of the station. In time, with practice, we can learn to not allow certain thoughts that trigger negative emotions to take hold, and rather to give our attention to other thoughts. It's as simple as this: we are not our thoughts. If you're not familiar with this type of mindfulness thinking, that may come as a surprise. *"They're my thoughts and therefore I own them, right?"* The thoughts that enter your mind through your subconscious are not controlled by you, but your conscious mind has the power to do with them what you wish.

Self-control extends far beyond what we think, of course, because our thoughts impact our emotional state and the actions we choose to take. Equally important are the actions we choose not to take. Perhaps you've experienced the following sequence.

You read an email from a work colleague and you detect a nasty tone. You feel as though you are being attacked and you immediately become agitated and decide to yourself that you're not going to take this insult lying down. You draft an email that clarifies a few things, declares that you don't deserve nor will you accept the aggressive tone you've detect and you even go so far as to explain that this is not the first time you've been spoken to in a way that you feel is unprofessional. You're about to hit send and you stop and give it another thought.

Look at you, demonstrating self-control. Hopefully, here's what happens next. You, being a mature person, consider what you'll achieve by sending this email. It may provoke a defensive or aggressive response. Knowing this colleague as well as you do, your confidence in his ability to take constructive criticism is low. As you pause and take into account the shortcomings of the individual you were about to engage in a less than optimal manner, you begin to calm down.

The words that triggered you and made you want to shoot back with an equally venomous attack are words that you now recognize are the words you associate with something bigger that sticks in your craw, but that you can rise above reacting to. You send back a polite response that clarifies the issue without responding to the tone of the email you received. It feels good. Maturity, self-control and discipline at work!

Apply, Rinse and Repeat

Discipline is quite possibly the best tool we have in our "Build An Outstanding Human" toolbox. It can be applied anywhere. Discipline is not just for showing up on time, saying no to dessert, or working overtime. Discipline can be applied to the process required for finding creative solutions, maintaining healthy relationships, and even regulating our emotions. You name it, discipline can fix it or improve it. With such a potent tool at your disposal, why wouldn't we apply it liberally? You wouldn't be wrong to think "I'm going to dust off my discipline and use it everywhere I can." The question isn't should you, it's can you? There's a reason so much of this book is devoted to finding and sustaining motivation and being prepared for the highs and lows that come with the calls for motivation that come back to us unanswered. Like most valuable things, discipline comes with a high price.

The price of discipline is focus, determination and courage. If you have a wealth of these qualities, you can afford a sizable discipline practice. If you find yourself disappointed with your reserve of these qualities, no worries. Discipline provides a positive return on investment. In other words, using whatever focus, determination, and courage you have currently is enough to work with. Use it and put discipline to work for you. Discipline always pays a dividend, so the more you use it, the more focus, determination, and courage you'll find growing in your reserves. It's a cycle of positivity.

Discipline on Demand

What's the best part of our new-ish "on demand" societal evolution? The intention is certainly that we have what we want delivered, when we need it. Discipline is always ready for what's next. We don't call on it more often than we need because we know it comes with strings attached. We actually call on it less often than we need it for this reason. Discipline is powerful, but it also has power over us. It requires a commitment and some of us are commitment-phobic. Commitments limit our flexibility. Making a commitment means being accountable. What if I change my mind? Can I cancel my order for discipline? *Not without a penalty.*

Now you see why we talk about maturity. Yes, being accountable means that we don't always leave our options open to see if there's something we might want to commit to instead. There comes a time when the right decision is to commit to what we want – and lock it in. If we let our fear of commitment stand in the way, time passes, and it's not a zero-sum game, it's a lost opportunity.

Because we have discipline on demand, at the ready, it's our obligation to use it or lose it, quite literally. Remember how important muscle memory is for making any process work better with less energy applied. We humans don't have an infinite amount of energy to throw at our endeavors. As a result, we owe it to ourselves to incorporate discipline into our lives as often as possible. Discipline is a two-way street. Give it your strength via commitment and it will provide you with strength by way of its straightforward nature. Life can get awfully confusing sometimes, and discipline is that North Star we can count on for unfailing guidance. Discipline is always the right answer to any perplexing problem we encounter.

Foresight, Follow-Through, and Follow-Up

If there's one thing we know about discipline, it's that it doesn't work passively. To harness the power of discipline, it needs to be part of your plan and part of your process. When you put together you plan for goal achievement, a best practice is to include discipline by name. All too often we think to ourselves "Of course I'll need to be disciplined to make this work," but we leave it there. If you want to be able to call on it for strength, give it the strength of attention and intention. Make it clear to yourself that discipline isn't an afterthought, but a center of focus. If you were budgeting for a car trip, you would surely include gas as a line item. If discipline is a necessity, include it in the plan. This way you prepare your mind to bring the energy needed for a disciplined approach to your process.

Within your process, honor discipline rather than taking it for granted. Be grateful to yourself for making discipline a priority and grateful for the power that comes from discipline. You could be doing a great number of other things right now, but you're focused on discipline, and you have discipline to thank for that focus. Being attentive to what's important to you is an increasingly valuable discipline in our modern world, which is full of so many distractions, some worthy and some not. Just as the time you spend planning is valuable, so too is the time you spend evaluating your process. Yes, you want to *trust the process*, which alludes to the point that you've made a good plan and no need to overthink, *just do it*. That's great for digging in each day, but it's also important to evaluate the outcomes because there's a difference between overthinking and thinking. Be sure to give thought to what you can do to improve your process. Become more efficient and, as your capabilities grow, perhaps even more demanding of yourself.

Follow-through is another concept you may want to keep top of mind within your process. Think about different techniques you've learned thus far. How important is follow-through for producing an optimal result? To hit a golf ball, a baseball or tennis ball well depends on follow-through. Applying for a job and succeeding in the interview process rely on follow-through for best results too. Slicing bread, throwing a party, and on and on, we could find example after example of actions we take where follow-through is not an afterthought, it's built into the process because it's that important. Discipline gives us the power to follow-through so that our process is complete.

Discipline and Mental Toughness

Here's a chicken and egg consideration: Does discipline fuel mental toughness, or is it mental toughness that fuels discipline? The answer is that, like the chicken and egg, each creates the other in an endless cycle, and it's unlikely that an undisputed answer as to which came first will ever be available to us. With regard to our concern, discipline and mental toughness, what's important is that we value the relationship.

Discipline and mental toughness are so closely related, you may simply think of them as the same thing. However, there is a distinction between the two that may prove helpful for consideration. Let's take for example that you find the discipline to get up early each morning and exercise before work. This demonstration of discipline is impressive, as you value your sleep and getting up early is a sacrifice. You do it because you find that it makes you feel good. It relieves stress and offers a sense of clarity to start your day. Yes, there's a degree of mental toughness required to begin and sustain this routine. Once it becomes a routine, it becomes a healthy habit and discipline that takes less energy, less mental toughness to follow-through.

When a new project at work requires extra time to complete, you may consider the option of foregoing your morning workout to put that time into the work project. This is where mental toughness comes into play. You've established a discipline that is rewarding, but you have a conflict between competing needs for that time, and it's your mental toughness that allows you to temporarily alter your routine, skipping your morning exercise for a period of time to adjust for another high priority activity. This distinction between mental toughness and discipline may be "splitting hairs," because once again, the two are so closely related.
Certainly, it's mental toughness that we summon to commit to being disciplined in any given area in our life. It's also mental toughness that we call on to evaluate whether our discipline in one part of life is causing us to be inflexible or imbalanced

when new life events cause us to reevaluate our actions. Life is full of hard decisions to be made. Being mentally tough allows us to confront tough decisions and not kick them down the road to be confronted another day. It provides us with the determination to stay focused on those things we deem most important in our life, including what it takes to embrace discipline for the sake of efficiency and progress.

You may want to consider mental toughness as sitting above discipline, along with the other characteristics you want to foster and grow. There are times when the servant leads the master. Do think about the ways you can use discipline to strengthen your mental toughness. Discipline is a great task master. When your mental toughness needs support, use discipline to ensure that important decisions are made in a timely manner and that procrastination is minimized. Employ discipline to embrace mindfulness practices that help you regulate your emotional state, and in doing so you strengthen your mind and give your mental toughness room to grow.

Mental toughness is about more than being disciplined and holding your feet to the fire. Mental toughness can be called upon to treat yourself, and others with compassion. It can be what you use to be mindful of the importance that balance plays in your life. Mental toughness can be called upon when you need to become more aggressive, but be sure not to confuse mental toughness with aggressiveness because of your common association with the work tough.
Mental toughness is what allows us to be our best self - to be brave, kind, vulnerable, powerful, caring, prepared, optimistic, honest and disciplined.

Mastering discipline requires that first and foremost you are prepared to make good on the promises you make to yourself. You will master discipline when you apply your best effort; nurture your motivation, acknowledge your accomplishments, forgive yourself when you fall short and always be ready to begin again. Discipline is a practice. Perfection is not possible, but mastery sure is.

Conclusion

Commanding a life full of so much potential is a big responsibility. Without a good game plan, it can be downright overwhelming. If you find yourself at a crossroad, this is a good place to begin again. If you feel like you could do a better job navigating life's waters, no worries. You are here for a reason and you can employ a strategy that meets you exactly where you're at right now.

Discipline is a big issue. This book was crafted to look at it from all angles, to go deep and to gain understanding about what motivates us and what holds us back. At the end of the day, it's really those opposing forces at work that lead us down the paths we choose.

The intention of this book is to make discipline more approachable. Not just for the sake of trying to do better, but because starting is often the most difficult part of any journey. This book is also full of intention to demystify discipline. To find the answers to questions about why some people seem to find discipline so easy, while others find it almost impossible. Like anything you pursue, once you understand it, you're more than halfway there.

Understanding discipline means understanding the forces at play. Understanding all the ways our mind throws up roadblocks. Understanding how negative thinking keeps us on the sidelines when we're yearning to get into the game. This same negative thinking is what derails us, if we allow it, once have made progress and gained momentum.

Without discipline our focus comes and goes – and without focus our discipline does the same. We've explored how frequently our minds work in this cylindrical fashion. We've examined how these cycles can propel us when they are based on positivity and conversely how they set us back when fueled by negative thinking.

It's evident to see how discipline = power. We look around and see people who harness the power of discipline to accomplish their goals and live their dreams. We know that the people who do this, people who we admire for it, are just like us. They're not superhuman. They've simply mastered what it takes to put the practice of discipline into place and to work it.

You know that when your motivations and values are aligned that you can be disciplined without feeling like you're pushing a rock uphill. You know that this is secret. This is how people do it. The energy required to sustain your discipline diminishes once you make momentum work for you, and you build muscle memory.

You know that success breeds success because there's nothing more powerful than feeling confident. Experience has taught you that confidence is what's needed to initiate a new practice – and to address a practice of discipline as if you're addressing it for the first time. This is the first time because you've never tried it before being the person you are today.

You now know more about the inner workings of discipline. You know that your drive is anchored by the promises you make to yourself. You know that you are brave enough to commit, and to be accountable for decisions. You know that this level of accountability makes you feel vulnerable and that being vulnerable is part of solving this puzzle.

You realize that you can only make a promise and commit if you're willing to fail. You also know that failure is not an option for you because you can only fail if you quit. You choose not to quit. You see setbacks, not failure. You know that what some perceive as failure is what you perceive as having not succeeded yet. You know that every attempt teaches you something and gets you closer to achieving your goals.

You are ready to embrace discipline to master self-control and create better habits. You know the value of planning. Not just to provide the road map that will enable you to achieve your goal, but to prepare you for the obstacles that will undeniably reveal themselves. This is real life and the game changes as you move along.

You know that obstacles will arise from external forces. Unforeseen events will threaten to move your discipline practice off course. You also know that the toughest obstacles will arise from within you. Your planning will ready you for the negative thoughts that will undoubtedly arise from your self-conscious mind. You'll acknowledge the presence of these thoughts but place your attention elsewhere.

Discipline empowers you to control your attention and your intention. Your discipline practice will strengthen your mental toughness and provide you with a greater degree of self-control.

With your newfound understanding of discipline, you realize that you do own discipline. You always have. You've always exercised it in certain areas of your life and not in others. You realize that what's held you back from applying it elsewhere was your fear of failure.

You recognize that no achievement worth being proud of is accomplished without tackling the fear of failure. Now it seems so obvious that you can't be "in the game" and pursue success without accepting that failure part of the equation. You also know that your ability to commit, your courage and your determination won't allow you to truly fail, regardless of any outcome.

This is your time. With so much potential and so many skills, all that's missing is a healthy dose of discipline. You realize that your discipline practice will take center stage in your game plan from now on. You empower discipline with your attention and discipline empowers you – it's as good a relationship as you could ask for.

With discipline on your side, you are unstoppable. You've envisioned what it looks like and feels like to live your life with discipline, and if feels pretty darn good.

Discipline is one of the few things in life that you can count on to provide you with a positive return on your investment.

Give discipline your attention, your intention and your energy and you'll be thrilled with what you get back. Discipline is powerful, but it won't come find you and initiate the practice. **It begins with you.**

www.ingramcontent.com/pod-product-compliance
Lightning Source LLC
Chambersburg PA
CBHW071450070526
44578CB00001B/292